POLICE CULTURE

POLICE CULTURE

ADAPTING TO THE STRAINS OF THE JOB

Eugene A. Paoline III
UNIVERSITY OF CENTRAL FLORIDA

William Terrill
MICHIGAN STATE UNIVERSITY

CAROLINA ACADEMIC PRESS
Durham, North Carolina

Library of Congress Cataloging-in-Publication Data

Paoline, Eugene A.
  Police culture : adapting to the strains of the job / Eugene Paoline and William Terrill.
       pages cm
  Includes bibliographical references and index.
  ISBN 978-1-61163-047-3 (alk. paper)
  1. Police--United States--Attitudes. 2. Police subculture--United States. 3. Police--Job stress--United States. I. Terrill, William, 1965- II. Title.

  HV8138.P367 2013
  305.9'36320973--dc23

                          2013030667

Carolina Academic Press
700 Kent Street
Durham, North Carolina 27701
Telephone (919) 489-7486
Fax (919) 493-5668
www.cap-press.com

Printed in the United States of America
2019 Printing

Contents

Introduction

Having taught thousands of students, and interacted with policing scholars and practitioners from all parts of the United States, a highly identifiable topic of discussion is police culture. Broad-based terms such as *thin blue line, brotherhood,* and *blue code of silence* are used to characterize the collective bond that police officers share. At the same time, while many are comfortable talking about police culture, a large degree of vagueness and confusion comes with this concept. Similar to the notion of love, if you survey a hundred people asking them to explain police culture, you are liable to get a hundred different responses. These responses would undoubtedly include a variety of definitions, causes and consequences, and levels of aggregation. It is probably not a coincidence that researchers who have tackled the "culture beast" often write a single book, article, or chapter and then venture off to another area of inquiry. As such, one primary aim of this book is to provide a working definition of police culture while organizing the disparate conceptualizations that currently exist.

From a research standpoint, a large portion of what we "know" about police culture is based on single-agency ethnographic studies conducted over a half century ago. These works focused on qualitatively detailing commonalities (at the expense of potential differences) among police officers. Debates over the existence of a single police culture versus various cultural adaptations were born primarily out of patrol officer typology studies. Such works collectively spanned several police departments, often mixing qualitative and quantitative methods to empirically refute the idea of a single police culture in illustrating different policing styles. In large part, the impetus for these inquiries was based on the search for the "professional" style, following a time when the Supreme Court was placing limits on the crime fighting mandates espoused by the reform era of policing. Additional works have highlighted cultural segmentation among officers based on factors such as the differing type of police organizations and rank designations. More recent inquiries have been geared toward the development of quantitatively based classification schemes, which in many ways resemble typology studies. A key distinction is that these works rely less on rich descriptive detail and focus more on the statistical modeling and advanced analytical techniques employed. Like typology approaches before them, these studies were also a result of changes that occurred in policing (i.e., police officer demographics and post-professionalization organizational philosophies).

Despite additions that highlight segmentation, the prevailing view of the police is that they are bound by a single culture (which is described in a variety of ways) regardless of where and for whom they work. This often results in scholars taking sides between the popular characterization of the police as a single "brotherhood" and those who believe that the collectiveness has been overstated. In the end, the knowledge base has suffered, since researchers have been caught up purely in the "homogeneity versus heterogeneity" debate. Logically, there are probably dimensions of culture that officers share, but there are also cultural features that exhibit variation among officers, especially in an ever-changing police world. From an empirical standpoint, we have yet to fully explore such dynamics. As such, a second primary aim of this book is to empirically revisit some of the foundational elements of police culture. In doing so, we assess officers' cultural views across seven police agencies of varying size, structure, and geographic locales, within a post-community policing work environment.

Chapter 1 provides a comprehensive review of police culture, which should allow readers to walk away with a clear understanding of the various conceptualizations of police culture and how research from each perspective has been conducted. The second chapter offers a historical look at American policing in terms of ideological approaches, operational strategies, and police culture. As part of this discussion, we examine how recent changes in policing (e.g., evidence-based policing) mirror past approaches, and what we can learn from this history with respect to police culture. Chapter 3 outlines the environmental features of our seven study sites. We begin by discussing the external environments in relation to how the cities were situated (e.g., population, crime, arrests, etc.), and then provide an organizational sketch of each police department by detailing how the agencies were organized and structured, as well as the policies and supervisory procedures that were in operation—all of which have implications for understanding police culture.

Chapter 4 describes the survey research process and highlights important lessons from the field. We focus on elements such as coordinating the survey of groups of patrol officers, the importance of gaining cooperation from upper level and middle management, presenting the study goals and objectives in person, obtaining consent from research participants, and dealing with confidentiality and anonymity concerns. In the fifth chapter, we assess patrol officer perceptions of their internal (i.e., the police department) and external (i.e., the street) work environments. In particular, we look closely at the ways in which police officers deal with the various strains of the job in either similar or disparate ways, as well as the extent to which officers embody the cumulative values of the occupational culture perspective. In the final chapter we summarize key findings from the study, discuss the implications of this work, and speculate on the future of police culture research.

Suggested Reading Tips

This book is intended for audiences of various interests and knowledge levels. We surmise that Chapter 1 will appeal to most readers as it lays the foundation for understanding police culture from both a conceptual and research-based perspective. Beyond the initial chapter, readers may wish to be more discriminating based on their interests and existing knowledge of policing and culture. For undergraduates or students new to the policing literature, we would strongly suggest Chapter 2 as it offers a fairly succinct summary of the primary policing eras over the past several hundred years, with an eye toward the role of culture. More advanced students, researchers, scholars, and practitioners may already have a good grip on these historical components and decide to skim this chapter and concentrate on other chapters of interest. Chapter 3 offers perhaps the most comprehensive description of study sites found within the policing literature. In doing so, we go into significant detail on each of the seven organizations. Those interested in organizations from any number of angles, including but also well beyond culture, should find this chapter worthwhile, while those with a more casual interest in the topic need not get caught up in some of the minutia. One can certainly browse this chapter and not be lost in the later chapters.

While Chapter 3 may be ideal for readers who focus on organizations, Chapter 4 should be especially helpful for those with an interest in survey research. Beyond detailing the survey methodology for the present study, we offer many tips and insights for researchers interested in this methodological approach to social science research. Ph.D. students in particular may get quite a bit out of this chapter. Chapter 5 serves as the empirical glue that holds the book together. While not overly complicated in terms of sophisticated statistical analyses (i.e., descriptive in nature), we examine each culture element across the seven study agencies. In essence, Chapter 5 tells us what we uncovered in the study regarding facets of occupational culture police officers widely share and parts they do not. Finally, Chapter 6 offers a summary assessment of key findings, shedding light on contemporary police culture as well as the future of this area of inquiry. In this sense, we believe that readers of all levels of interest and knowledge will find this chapter worth reading.

In closing, readers should feel quite comfortable picking and choosing those chapters that appeal most to them, and concentrating less on those that do not. In this sense, the book is not written in a strictly linear fashion *per se*. We believe advanced readers can hone in on Chapters 1, 5, and 6 and still walk away with quite a bit. Undergraduates or students new to the topic may want to spend more time on the early chapters to get a feel for culture as a whole, and how it fits into the realm of policing over time, before tackling the later chapters. Yet policing generalists may have little interest in culture, but may still get quite a lot out of Chapter 3 (i.e., organizations) or Chapter 4 (i.e., survey research methodology) separate and apart from the remaining chapters. Of course we are also cognizant that some readers may not wish to delve into the level of detail such a book brings, and thus are simply interested in going directly to the concluding chapter to uncover the "big picture." If so, we say have at it, although as with any author, we would always prefer one reading more over less!

POLICE CULTURE

Chapter 1

Police Culture: Making Sense of Disparate Conceptualizations

Perhaps the best way to illustrate the confusion associated with the police culture area is by relaying the personal experiences, as a graduate student, of one of the authors of this book. Having been extensively trained in criminology (i.e., the study of crime), I fully understood the inherent abstract nature of concepts. In some ways, this prepared me for what I was to experience in choosing and conducting a doctoral dissertation on police culture, while in other respects it added to my frustration.

My transition to the study of criminal justice (over criminology) was largely a serendipitous one. Put simply, an accident. In need of continued graduate funding, I was approached to be a supervisor of a large-scale systematic social observation study of police (the Project on Policing Neighborhoods—POPN). At the time, like many criminologists, I viewed policing as a theoretically void applied area. As such, I respectfully declined the offer. Upon a bit more prodding, I agreed to join the project, almost entirely because a criminology pioneer, Al Reiss, Jr., was a co-principal investigator. I naively believed that this would be a worthwhile opportunity, even if only for a few discussions with Reiss. Looking back now, I am embarrassed of such a myopic view of the academic field, as I am fully entrenched in police research. Moreover, from this project, several doors were opened for me, I gained a mentor, and I met my closest friend, research collaborator, and co-author of this book.

Fast forward three years—the POPN field work, required courses, and comprehensive finals were all complete; it was time to sketch out a definitive dissertation plan. Following several meetings with my dissertation chair, I ultimately decided that I would conduct a study on police culture. In my estimation, this was the closest that I could get to my criminology roots, as culture is a prominent feature of several theories of crime. Unfortunately, when I started to conduct a review of the literature, I could not locate the theoretical assumptions, propositions, or the causal model for police culture. I quickly realized that unlike Strain (Merton, 1938), Social Disorganization (Shaw & McKay, 1942), and Culture Conflict (Sellin, 1938) theories, a nice and tidy clear-cut foundation, with a path of empirical tests and theoretical revisions, was not available.

For more than six months, I read everything and anything that mentioned police culture. This is when I fully realized the lack of cohesion and the various disparate conceptualizations. Further muddying the waters was a series of interchangeable terms (e.g., culture/subculture, occupational/organizational culture, subculture/styles, etc.), varying (or lack of agreed upon) definitions, mixed levels of aggregation, and different connotations (i.e., good versus bad). It appeared as if police culture was used as a matter of convenience, and as if the reader was to have an *a priori* comprehension of the manner in which the researcher was using the term. It was not as if those writing about the topic were wrong; it was just that the explanations appeared to be all over the place. It was at this time that I started (and continue) to organize the various conceptualizations of police culture, if for nothing else than to assist others who find themselves in the predicament I was in. What follows is a discussion of the various ways in which police culture has been described, as well as a clear way to distinguish one perspective from another.

Defining Culture

Before addressing the ways in which police culture has been conceptualized, we begin by operationalizing *culture*. Societies, occupations, agencies, units, workgroups all, in varying degrees, have culture. Those who have studied culture across these different levels of aggregation have provided a variety of definitions of this phenomenon. A few illustrative examples include:

> … it denotes a historically transmitted pattern of meanings embodied in symbols, a system of inherent conceptions expressed in symbolic forms by means of which men communicate, perpetuate, and develop their knowledge about and attitudes toward life (Geertz, 1973, p. 89).

> An occupational culture is a reduced, selective, and task-based version of culture that is shaped by and shapes the socially relevant worlds of the occupation (Manning, 1995, p. 472).

A pattern of shared basic assumptions that the group learned as it solved its problems of external adaption and internal integration, that has worked well enough to be considered valid and, therefore, to be taught to new members as the correct way to perceive, think, and feel in relation to those problems (Schein, 1992, p. 12).

... culture embodies the identity of the social group. What we, as members, stand for and how we deal with one another and with outsiders is carried in and through our culture (Louis, 1983, p. 44).

... culture can be understood as a set of solutions devised by a group of people to meet specific problems posed by situations they face in common (Van Maanen & Barley, 1985, p. 33).

Across each of these definitions, which span a host of research arenas, a set of common themes emerges. First, culture is a shared group phenomenon. In addition, the attitudes, values, and norms that constitute culture assist group members in dealing with problematic conditions that arise whether it is in life, one's job, one's organization, or some other unit of analysis. Finally, culture is transmitted across members through a socialization (i.e., teaching and learning) process. As such, *culture comprises the attitudes, values, and norms that are transmitted and shared among groups of individuals in an effort to collectively cope with the common problems and conditions members face.* The specific attitudes, values, and norms, the various levels of aggregation (i.e., occupation, organization, subgroup), and the degree of sharedness, have all been part of the various cultural accounts of police.

Disparate Conceptualizations of Police Culture

In "making sense" of disparate conceptualizations of police culture, we concentrate on four primary areas, which also represent different units of analysis with varying cultural assumptions. We begin with (1) *occupational* accounts, as this represents the loose framework for the majority of ideas and writings on this subject matter (i.e., either in attempting to explain or refute it), and as such more attention is given to this explanation of police culture. This is also the area that produces the most confusion, as a variety of concepts and ideas have been used to capture "the" police culture. Paoline's (2003) conceptual model is utilized to organize the various works that encompass occupational accounts, which serves as a point of departure for the three other explanations that highlight cultural variation based on different units of analysis that include policing (2) *organizations*, (3) *ranks*, and (4) *styles*. Across each of these four different levels of aggregation, we summarize the key assumptions, foundational research,[1] primary cultural explanation, and the common research methodologies employed.

Police Occupational Culture

By far, the most popular conception and aggregation of police culture is from the occupational level. When one opens an introductory policing textbook or a peer reviewed journal, or reads a news publication about the police, with any mention of culture, the occupational version is what they are most likely referring to. This is represented as a collective bond and professional world-view that arises among police officers as a result of the common strains encountered on the job. In revisiting the aforementioned definition, the police occupational culture consists of the attitudes, values, and norms that are transmitted and shared among officers in an effort to collectively cope with the problems and conditions they face as members of the police profession. Such accounts of culture are not just reserved for policing, as virtually all occupations develop and sustain some form(s) of culture (Van Maanen & Barley, 1984). What we find in descriptions of police culture, from the occupational point of view, is a series of writings that attempt to characterize the various features and strains encountered in the policing environments, as well as the cultural responses endorsed in buffering such strains. Common references to the occupational culture refer to it as the "traditional" or "monolithic" account of police culture (Paoline, 2003).

Key Assumptions

Proponents of the police occupational culture perspective assume that there is just one (i.e., monolithic) culture. In a related manner, occupational accounts of police culture assume homogeneity among officers no matter where, when, and for whom they work. That is, "a cop is a cop" and the conditions of the work environments are the same whether they work in New York, Florida, Michigan, or California, thus the cultural reaction will be the same. Another assumption from this perspective is that culture originates and is maintained and transmitted by lower level participants during their time on patrol.

---

1. We caution the reader that across the four classifications of police culture we are not providing a comprehensive list of all research and writings conducted, but instead those that best capture (and illustrate) the core ideas of each area. In doing so, we focus on works done in the United States so as to not confound cultural dynamics that might exist across internationally diverse police agencies and communities.

It is assumed that because all police start at this introductory level that *this* is where culture takes place. Once officers leave patrol they still carry some degree of their cultural values with them, but the heart of this perspective focuses on the street-level police officer. Moreover, culture is viewed as less of a function of what you bring to the profession, in terms of your background, orientations, and demographics, and much more about how the police occupation itself shapes you (Van Maanen, 1974).

Foundational Research

Two seminal sociological studies of police serve as the foundation for the occupational police culture perspective. The first is William Westley's (1970) doctoral research in the early 1950s, and the second is Jerome Skolnick's (1966) work in the early 1960s. Neither set out to study police culture *per se*, but they both provide rich ethnographic detail on the environments that police work within, and the collectiveness that is formed among police as they adapt to occupational challenges. These works are the core for understanding the occupational account of police culture, and have provided a broad framework for others to contribute to the discussion of the working conditions that police officers encounter and the collective adaptations that develop.

Westley's (1970) research, in Gary, Indiana, was the first to pick up on a variety of occupational culture themes, especially in terms of relationships that exist between police and citizens as well as between police and other officers. With respect to external interactions between officers and citizens, Westley reported a high degree of reciprocal violence and hostility between the two groups. The noted violence and hostility in the street-based work environment resulted in the routine use of aggressive third-degree practices by police officers. Westley explained that officers were taught such techniques by senior personnel through an informal socialization process. The noted negative relationship between police and citizens also worked to strengthen a collective bond among police, as they socially isolated themselves from outsiders (e.g., citizens, media, researchers, etc.). Such secrecy and loyalty were so strong that Westley found that more than 75% (of a sample of 15 officers) admitted that they would perjure themselves in court in order to protect a fellow officer (1970, p. 113). Cumulatively, this initial occupational culture research highlighted a high degree of tension between police and citizens (on the street) and strong inter-group cohesion among officers.

Another seminal police study by Skolnick (1966) added to the work of Westley (1970) in forming our initial impressions of the occupational culture perspective. Skolnick, based on research in Oakland, California, explained that police occupational culture was characterized by a distinct working personality that was a result of three primary features of the job. The first two elements of the police personality were a product of the occupational street environment and the interactions that officers have with citizens. Skolnick noted, in a similar way as Westley (1970) did a decade earlier, that the streets that occupational members police are characterized by *danger*, where officers wield a tremendous amount of *authority* over citizens. Central to this explanation was the fact that Skolnick asserted that it was not as if certain types of individuals (e.g., authoritarian) were being attracted to (or recruited into) policing, but that the police personality developed as a function of the conditions that occupational members confront on the job. The author also identified a third primary component that helped create the working personality: the need to appear *efficient* in the eyes of supervisors. Such a mandate was understandable, given the 20th century professional reform movement (see Chapter 2), although the interpretation set forth by Skolnick was that such mandates contributed to tension between officers and their bosses. In adding to Westley's work, Skolnick introduced an equally dangerous and hostile work environment as that on the street in dealing with citizens, the police organization, and the interactions that officers have with supervisors.

Primary Cultural Explanation

Westley (1970) and Skolnick's (1966) research identified the problematic conditions that exist across the primary external (i.e., street) and internal (i.e., organization) environments that police work within, as well as the occupational collectiveness and isolation (from outsiders) that results. For several decades that followed, researchers identified and described additional features of these two work environments, as well as the shared consequences and outcomes of working on the street and within the police organization. While all of this work has implications for understanding the occupational culture of police, the sum of the individual parts was left up to the reader. That is, police researchers and scholars would individually focus on factors such as: *danger* (e.g., Barker, 1999; Cullen, Link, Travis, & Lemming, 1983; Herbert, 1998; Toch, 1973; Van Maanen, 1978), *coercive power* (e.g., Banton, 1964; Bittner, 1967, 1970, 1974; Chevigny, 1969; Muir, 1977), *social isolation* (e.g., Drummond, 1976; Kelling & Kliesmet, 1996; Niederhoffer, 1967; Rubinstein, 1973; Sparrow, Moore, & Kennedy, 1990); *loyalty* (e.g., Brown, 1988; Drummond, 1976; Reuss-Ianni, 1983; Rubinstein, 1973; Van Maanen, 1974), *CYA/supervisors* (e.g., Crank; 1997; Herbert, 1996; McNamara, 1967; Reuss-Ianni, 1983; Van Maanen, 1974), and *crime fighter role orientation* (e.g., Bittner, 1974; Jermier, Slocum, Fry, & Gaines, 1991; Klockars, 1985; Rumbaut & Bittner, 1979; Sparrow et al., 1990), all under the umbrella of police culture, leaving out how each of these numerous cultural elements related to one another in a causal manner. Paoline's (2003) *Monolithic Police Culture Model* helped alleviate such concerns by providing a description (based on extant research) of how the stressful features of the primary work environments produce collective prescriptive coping mechanisms and outcomes. In doing so, this model serves as a template for understanding the primary explanation of culture per the occupational perspective.

In a path-like presentation, Paoline (2003) identifies interactions on the street with citizens (i.e., *occupational*) and those with supervisors in the department (i.e., *organizational*) as the two primary work environments of the police. As a starting point for understanding what produces the coping mechanisms of the monolithic culture, the occupational street environment is described as *dangerous*, with the defining mandate to display one's *coercive authority* over citizens. The model also details the organizational environment as being characterized by uncertain *supervisor scrutiny* of police decisions (i.e., watchful and punitive superiors) and *role ambiguity* whereby officers are expected to perform all police functions equally, yet really only are recognized for crime fighting duties. Both the occupational and organizational environments produce equally intense stress and anxiety that is relieved through the collective coping mechanisms found within the occupational police culture.

In illustrating the second principal feature of the monolithic police culture model, Paoline (2003) identifies *suspiciousness* (in minimizing the potential for danger) and *maintaining the edge* (in properly displaying coercive power) as the primary coping mechanisms that officers employ in handling the strains created on the street with citizens. In terms of dealing with supervisors within the equally hostile organizational environment, the culture prescribes that officers *lay low/CYA* (from watchful and punitive superiors) and embrace the *crime fighter orientation* (in minimizing role ambiguity, as training, commendations, and promotions are usually reserved for such functions). These prescriptive coping mechanisms of the police occupational culture are transmitted across officers via a socialization process that formally begins in the training academy and continues throughout one's career (Van Maanen, 1974). The final stage of the model highlights the consequences of the strains of the work environments and the coping mechanisms endorsed by the culture, which include a *socially isolated* (from citizens) occupational group that is extremely *loyal* to fellow officers.

Collectively, the work that helped produce this model paints a caricature sketch of police as socially isolated, distrustful, and suspicious of their primary clientele, as they continually attempt to maintain the upper hand in utilizing their coercive authority in a dangerous world. Moreover, officers approach police work solely in crime fighting terms, while laying low from punitive-minded supervisors, choosing to trust only their immediate peers.

Common Research Methodologies

Among those who endorse the occupational perspective of police culture, we find an emphasis on qualitatively based ethnographic research methods. Such an approach, an anthropological one common among many cultural studies beyond policing, utilizes unstructured observations and open-ended interviews of research subjects (Patton, 2002, p. 81). These methods are also routinely supplemented with a snowball sampling method where the researcher moves from subject to subject based on opportunities that present themselves in the field (e.g., a referral from a research participant or something witnessed while observing or interviewing). The aim of such methods is to capture, illustrate, and document common themes, which are usually utilized to develop hypotheses in unchartered study areas for others to systematically examine with additional research methodologies (e.g., structured social observations and surveys with predefined protocols). The use of ethnographic approaches, in seeking out commonalities, might also explain why those endorsing the occupational view of police culture highlight the central tendencies and similarities among officers versus cultural differences that might exist.

Police Organizational Culture

Another way that culture is conceptualized, and often confused as synonymous with occupational versions, is from the organizational level. A key distinction that separates the two is that organizational accounts assert that culture *does* vary across the occupation and is a function of where (and for whom) one works. In this sense, cultural explanations from the organizational standpoint seek to describe the collectiveness among officers working in a given agency as opposed to the entire police profession. For illustrative purposes, consider an officer who works for a department that is situated in a highly populated, crime ridden, urban area versus one who polices for an agency located in a moderately populated, low crime, suburban setting. The types of problematic conditions, to which officers are responding, should be vastly different for those working in the former over the latter. Moreover, the messages, missions, and expectations should also differ across these two contrasting organizational settings. As such, the resulting culture among police officers operating within these different work environments should also vary. This is the perspective that organizational culture proponents endorse.

Key Assumptions

Those who conceptualize culture from the organizational level assume that policing environments (i.e., organizational and occupational) differ as a function of some identifiable attributes that exist across police agencies. So, it is not so much the occupation itself (i.e., being a police officer) that produces culture, it is the specific agency, and the community it is situated within, that produces different organizationally derived cultures. Like the occupational versions of police culture, it is assumed that organizations will have one overriding culture, and thus there will be homogeneity in the outlooks and approaches of departmental personnel. As opposed to occupational accounts that assume that culture originates and is maintained by front-line personnel, organizational accounts assume that the top leader (i.e., chief, sheriff, commissioner) is an instrumental force that defines the culture for the entire police agency.

Foundational Research

The foundation for organizational accounts of police culture is based on the work of James Q. Wilson (1968). Wilson's study of organizational culture, which he believed was reflective of an overall departmental style, examined eight non-southern policing communities in the mid-to-late 1960s. Wilson identified three organizational styles that differed from one another primarily by their prioritization of core policing role orientations related to enforcing the law and maintaining order. Wilson asserted that the top administrator (i.e., chief, superintendent, commissioner, or captain), in filtering the primary needs of the community being served (i.e., political culture), establishes the organizational culture for others to follow.

According to Wilson (1968), some departments are situated within urban environments characterized by greater crime concerns, and thus the agency will embrace more of a formal crime fighting detached approach to police work. In such *legalistic* style departments, arrests and tickets will be more frequent (and expected) compared to other organizational styles. By contrast, Wilson's *watchman* style departments are more common in low crime rural areas, focusing primarily on maintaining public order. Watchman style departments are less likely to formally respond to citizen transgressions unless they are serious in nature. Wilson asserted that the relational distance between the police and the public in watchman areas would be much closer than that found in legalistic style departments. Finally, *service* style departments are described by Wilson as those where law enforcement and order maintenance is not an overall priority, but would be handled as needed. These departments focus on providing assistance and are more likely to be situated in suburban areas with less crime and disorder. Wilson explained that service style departments are closely connected with citizens, choosing to intervene frequently (when needed) but not formally (e.g., arrests and tickets).

More recently, Hassell (2007), in considering the theoretical ideas set forth by Klinger (1997), extended the organizational culture framework by emphasizing the role of the precinct, which can operate as sub-organizations within an overall police department. This is especially true in larger decentralized jurisdictions that contain a number of precincts where officers are housed in different geographically located police stations. In this sense, attention is paid to the notion that policing areas (e.g., cities, municipalities, counties, etc.) are not characterized by single organizational (and occupational) environments, and as such, may have multiple departmental cultures across the precincts where officers are stationed.

Hassell's (2007) research examined four police precincts in a single Midwestern police department. Hassell found, across the precincts, differences in the street environments as well as the style of policing espoused by the top precinct commander (i.e., captain). For example, the Northeast (NE) precinct was described as the smallest in geographic size, but it housed the most officers. This precinct was characterized as the most violent and crime ridden, the poorest, and the one with the highest percentage of minority residents. The style prescribed by the precinct captain was that of a mixture of reactively handling the high volume of citizen calls, while at the same time proactively fighting crime. The Southeast (SE) precinct was similarly situated in terms of the external environment as the NE (i.e., violence, crime, and residential demographics), but the policing style endorsed by the captain differed in the sense that proactive crime fighting was reserved for only parts of the community. Interestingly, both of these precincts mirrored Wilson's (1968) legalistic style agencies, but operated at the sub-organizational unit of analysis.

By contrast, the Southwest (SW) precinct was described as the largest geographic area, yet housed the fewest number of officers. The environment being policed by this precinct was not dangerous, had the least amount of street crime, the highest income among residents, and the most traffic and alarm calls. The policing style endorsed in this precinct was to reactively handle citizen calls for service, where proactive crime fighting tactics were discouraged. In a similar vein, the Northwest (NW) precinct covered a large geographic area, with few officers, lower levels of crime, and high amounts of traffic and alarm calls. Compared to the SW, this area was more economically and demographically diverse, but much less than the NE and SE precincts. The precinct style endorsed by the captain was reactive, with some tolerance for proactive policing. Both the NW and SW precincts mirrored, in varying degrees, Wilson's service style organization.

Primary Cultural Explanation

The organizational perspective allows for cultural variation across different types of police departments and communities. Wilson's legalistic style departments, and Hassell's NE and SE precincts, represent internal and external environments that align with monolithic occupational accounts of police culture, and as such cultural prescriptions and outcomes toward citizens and supervisors would be similar. By contrast, the organizational and occupational environments found among watchman and service style (Hassell's NW and SW precincts) departments are dramatically different from legalistic ones. For example, the internal work arenas, with fewer bureaucratic controls, are not characterized by intense supervisor scrutiny and role ambiguity like that noted in occupational (and legalistic style) descriptions. Likewise, there is also stark variation in the occupational/street environments, as non-legalistic style areas are not overly hostile and crime-ridden, and officers are not isolated from the citizens they police. As such, cumulative coping mechanisms where officers are suspicious of (and maintain the edge over) citizens, strictly endorsing the crime fighter image, while covering their ass from supervisors, might be functional in a legalistic style department. However, this approach would be less likely, and probably not tolerated among upper level management, among the other divergent agency styles.

Common Research Methodologies

Similar to occupational accounts of police culture, researchers who focus on organizations as the unit of analysis often rely on unstructured interviews and observations with a variety of departmental members, especially those located at the very top and bottom of the organizational hierarchy. This allows researchers to get a qualitative sense of how culture is formed and transmitted from agency leaders through the organization to front-line personnel. Because comparisons are made across organizations, researchers also utilize structured survey methodologies, and work to standardize aspects of departmental visits in terms of time spent on site and with whom they interview, survey, and observe. Finally, approaches to understanding organizational culture are geared toward collecting a variety of official data (e.g., crime, arrests, tickets, calls for service, agency characteristics, population demographics, etc.) and organizational documents (e.g., standard operating procedures, policies,

newsletters, newspaper/historical accounts, etc.) from internal and external
sources in an effort to capture the official cultural nuances of the departments
(and communities) under study.

Police Rank Culture

Occupational versions of police culture focus on the homogeneity of attitudes,
values, and norms among members of the police profession, concentrating efforts heavily on the street-level patrol officer. The socialization process transmits
the culture across occupational members, and is often described as intense, especially for new personnel (Van Maanen, 1974). Because all police at some point
in their career are assigned to patrol functions, the supposition is that culture
originates at the lower ranks. In addition, the patrol level is where the majority
of a police department's personnel are located (Walker & Katz, 2008). Moreover,
across the police hierarchy, patrol officers are the ones who are most likely to
deal with citizens on the streets and with supervisors in the department. What
is much less clear is the role that culture plays in officers' lives once they move
beyond entry-level positions. For example, does the occupational culture buffer
the strains of the work environments for sergeants, lieutenants, captains, ma-
jors, deputy chiefs, and chiefs the same way(s) that it did for them when they
were on patrol, or do the disparate positions have different culture(s)? The rank
perspective helps answer such questions by describing culture as a product of
conditions unique to one's position in the organizational hierarchy.

Key Assumptions

Among those who conceive of culture from this orientation is an assumption that variation exists in the ways that police officers respond to the occupational world around them. That is, there is not just a single culture of police,
but instead police cultures. According to this approach, the primary source of
cultural differentiation among officers can be found in one's rank designation,
which produces different stressors and concerns that occupational members
collectively deal with. As such, culture originates and is maintained by members of various levels of the police chain of command. Finally, such rank related variation transcends organizational differences, as individual effects by
department are not noted.

Foundational Research

Two works serve as the base for rank conceptualizations of police culture.
The first, by Elizabeth Reuss-Ianni (1983), sketches a bifurcated police culture

where patrol officers are part of a "street cop culture" and upper level supervisors form a "management cop culture." A second piece, by Peter Manning (1994), helps fill in gaps between lower and upper level ranks by positing a trichotomized rank culture of "lower participants," "middle management," and "top command." Both Reuss-Ianni (1983) and Manning (1994) highlight the dynamic nature of police culture as changing and adapting to insulate group members' issues and concerns unique to their position in the organizational hierarchy.

Reuss-Ianni (1983), based on her research in two NYPD precincts, asserts that there are two distinct cultures in policing. The street cop culture, which the author delineates in a series of codes, focuses on the "here and now" daily grinds in policing. The codes of the street cop embody many of the values previously outlined as part of the police occupational culture, especially themes of peer loyalty (e.g., *watch out for your partner first and then the rest of the guys working that tour; don't give up another cop; hold up your end of the work; if you get caught off base, don't implicate anybody else*), laying low from supervisors (e.g., *be aggressive when you have to but don't be too eager; don't make waves; don't give them too much activity; keep out of the way of any boss from outside your precinct*), and cover-your-ass (e.g., *protect your ass; know your bosses*) (pp. 14–16).

Reuss-Ianni (1983) explains that a second culture, management cop culture, operates among supervisors, especially at the upper echelons. This culture focuses on city-wide long terms concerns (e.g., crime control, citizen responsiveness, organizational efficiency, etc.), factoring in a number of political, social, and economic elements. Reuss-Ianni contends that temporal changes in the dynamics of policing (e.g., officer composition, off-duty socialization patterns, resource competition, accountability concerns, etc.) have contributed to a dilution of the street cop culture of the prior times when organizational leaders could still utilize the codes of the street in running police agencies (pp. 1–4).

While it is easy to deduce that top commanders are embedded in the management cop culture and patrol officers operate within street cop culture, the culture guiding middle managers (i.e., sergeants and lieutenants), who may be in organizational limbo between the very bottom and the very top, is not as clear from Reuss-Ianni's work. Manning's (1994) work helps bring clarity to such vagueness.

Manning (1994), based on numerous years of extensive field work, also contends that police culture is hierarchically segmented, although he differentiates rank in a three tiered manner based on a series of themes and metathemes. At the first tier are *lower participants* (i.e., patrol and street sergeants) whose culture, like Reuss-Ianni's (1983) street cops, focuses on the immediate aspects of "real" police work. This culture is equivalent to the previously explained occupational account.

The author's second tier of culture focuses on *middle management* (i.e., some sergeants up to department brass) who emphasize supervisory control, but also concentrate heavily on buffering concerns of line members of the street (i.e., the first tier) and top police officials (i.e., the third tier). Manning (1994) points out that sergeants assigned to street functions can rest within the first tier (i.e., lower participant culture), while middle managers with other responsibilities beyond patrol may be part of the second tier. A similar argument was made by Van Maanen (1984) who differentiated between "street" and "station house" sergeants. Finally, *top command* culture (i.e., commanders, superintendents, deputy chiefs, chiefs) represents the third tier. Here, there is a concentration on dealing with the politics of running a police department internally, while also buffering the organization from external audiences.

Primary Cultural Explanation

The rank perspective, like occupational accounts, focuses on the internal and external conditions of policing that work to collectively bind members of various positions of the hierarchy. As such, culture is shaped and formed by one's rank designation. Reuss-Ianni's (1983) street cop and Manning's (1994) lower participant cultures are largely consistent with several of the themes of the occupational perspective synthesized by Paoline (2003). The primary contribution of the rank perspective lies in the discussion of culture beyond the entry-level formation among patrol officers, which is largely ignored by the occupational and organizational versions. As officers advance in rank to middle management and upper level command positions, conditions of the work environments change, and thus the cultural responses will be different from what helped members cope on the street during patrol assignments. At the furthest extreme (from patrol officers) are Reuss-Ianni's (1983) management cops and Manning's (1994) top command who are dealing with more aggregate level long-term concerns from a variety of internal and external audiences. Between such extremes are Manning's (1994) middle managers, who in some cases align more with street officers (i.e., with the strains created by interactions with citizens on the street and supervisors in the department), while in other instances mirror the culture prescribed by top management albeit at a lower level of aggregation.

Common Research Methodologies

Similar to occupational versions, those interested in capturing the cultural nuances across the various hierarchical divisions of the police organization utilize ethnographic techniques that emphasize unstructured observations and interviewing. Snowball sampling strategies are also employed based on opportunities that present themselves in the field. A key distinguishing feature of rank-related cultural studies is *where* the anthropological observations take place. While the external street environment helps paint a picture of the cultural landscape among officers, the internal organizational environment is equally, if not more, important, especially among ranks above the patrol level. As such, the interactions that police have with other supervisory, subordinate, and peer officers are a focal part of observational and interviewing methods utilized in rank-based studies of culture.

Police Styles

In addition to occupational, organizational, and rank accounts of police culture, is the notion that officers develop different working styles that are the product of the various ways in which they *individually* perceive central elements of their occupational (i.e., street) and organizational (i.e., supervisors) environments. As such, this version of police culture directly refutes the homogeneity in officer approaches to the job (i.e., all cops are the same) set forth by occupational accounts. To illustrate this line of thinking consider the routine traffic stop, the modal encounter that the average citizen has with a police officer. From a stylistic perspective, the decision as to whether to even engage in traffic enforcement, as part of one's role orientation, would be based on the officer's policing style. Moreover, of those who would pull over a motorist, the way in which the citizen was treated (e.g., detached, friendly, commanding, etc.) and how the stop was performed (e.g., business-like, aggressively, suspiciously, etc.), would all be a function of one's style. The officer style perspective became popularized based on a series of independent research inquiries conducted in the 1970s aimed at illuminating the extent to which officers embodied the values of the 20th century professional reform movement (White, 1972).

Key Assumptions

Those who endorse this perspective for understanding police culture, like occupational versions, assume that one's style develops primarily during their time on patrol. Also like occupational accounts of police culture, one's policing approach is less of a function of what one brings to the job, and instead is a result of the conditions of the work (i.e., the organizational and the street) itself. Unlike occupational (and line level rank) versions of culture, this account assumes that there is not just a single method of policing, but a variety of styles. As such, the supposition is that there are several ways to adapt to the strains of the work environments. Finally, officer styles transcend organizations, in that each of the policing approaches can be found in any of the various types of American police departments.

Foundational Research

In the 1970s, a series of studies identified a variety of police styles that directly oppose occupational depictions of police culture. Each of these independent works utilized different attitudinal dimensions to construct a working typology of police officers. For example, White (1972) focused on differentiating officers in terms of the application of techniques (i.e., particularistic or universalistic), whether officers were concerned with outcomes or processes, and if they were discretion-control or command-control oriented. In another approach, Broderick (1977) distinguished officers in terms of the degree to which they were concerned with maintaining social order (i.e., low or high) and due process of law (i.e., low or high). Muir's (1977) typology concentrated on separating officers' stylistic approaches to policing based on their ability to develop morality in exercising coercion or "passion" (i.e., integrated or conflicted) and "perspective" (i.e., tragic or cynical). While these studies cumulatively illustrated that officers differ in key components regarding what police culture is said to cover (e.g., dealings with citizens, role orientations, supervisor interactions, etc.), while also concluding with descriptions of virtually identical officer styles (despite utilizing different attitudinal dimensions to construct their typologies), they were not specifically addressing police culture in their work. So police culture inferences could be drawn from the collective nature of these studies, but such connections were largely left up to the reader. One approach that filled this gap was the typology research by Brown (1988).

Brown (1988) conducted his research in the early 1970s in three California police departments. The author directly addressed the role of culture and styles, explaining that collectively the police, as an occupational group, culturally demand that members are loyal to their peers, while at the same time the culture grants autonomy to individual officers in displaying their own working style (p. 85). Brown asserted that one's policing style develops as a function of attitudes toward two dimensions—aggressiveness and selectivity. Aggressiveness, according to Brown (p. 223), is "a matter of taking the initiative on the street to control crime and a preoccupation with order that legitimizes the use of illegal tactics," while selectivity "distinguishes those officers who believe that all laws should be enforced insofar as possible, and those who consciously assign felonies a higher priority." As such, officers vary in terms of being "high" or "low" in aggressiveness, and whether they are "selective" or "non-selective." Brown's four-fold typology identified an *old-style crime-fighter* style (i.e., high aggressiveness and selective), a *clean-beat crime-fighter* style (i.e., high aggressiveness and non-selective), a *service* style (i.e., low aggressiveness and selective), and a *professional* style (i.e., low aggressiveness and non-selective). Based on this research, Brown (p. 8) concluded that "patrolmen react in fundamentally different ways to the demands of their occupation, and rather than a common set of values and beliefs, what we find ... are highly distinctive approaches to police work."

The typology research of the 1970s illustrated important cultural segmentation among officers during a time when the occupational group was demographically homogenous (i.e., White males with a high school education), and working within a philosophical model of policing (i.e., professional) that stressed efficient crime fighting. Changes in the overall composition of police personnel (i.e., more females, non-Whites, and college education), as well as philosophies that stressed collaborative community-based approaches to police work (i.e., community policing) in the 1990s, prompted a revisitation to typology-like approaches. In doing so, a series of works (Cochran & Bromley, 2003; Jermier et al., 1991; Paoline, 2001, 2004), utilized advanced statistical techniques to examine more than just two or three attitudinal dimensions to classify groups of officers. Paoline's (2001, 2004) quantitatively driven classification scheme, which directly referred to prior typology work in setting expectations for group formation, provides one primary example.

Paoline's (2001, 2004) research combined many of the attitudinal constructs identified as part of occupational and officer style perspectives of culture (i.e., views toward citizens, supervisors, procedural guidelines, police role, and how the role should be performed), based on surveys of 585 patrol officers working within two demographically diverse departments that espoused community policing. Paoline found five groups of officers (*traditionalists, law enforcers, lay-lows, peacekeepers*, and *old-pros*) that closely resembled common styles noted in typology studies over two decades earlier. Paoline also identified two additional styles of officers that were not found in earlier typology research. One style was distinguished in terms of their strong negative perceptions of supervisors and their very favorably views of citizens (*anti-organizational street cops*), while another was noted for their overly positive beliefs in aggressively fighting crime and disorder, even if it meant bending the rules in violating the

rights of citizens (*dirty harry enforcers*). Again, like Brown's (1988) work, Paoline's (2001, 2004) research, during a different era of policing, illuminated
variation in the ways that officers responded to elements of their primary work
environments.

Primary Cultural Explanation

At the heart of the police styles perspective is the notion of cultural variation, which departs from the other two approaches that highlight segmentation (i.e., organizational and rank), while directly opposing occupational
monolithic versions. The contrast between this approach and occupational accounts is interesting in that there is partial support for the existence of the
adaptations noted in occupational versions of police culture. Worden's (1995)
synthesis of typology research, which was also used as a foundation for hypo-
thetical expectations in Paoline's (2001, 2004) contemporary extension of officer styles, illustrates such points.

Worden (1995), in synthesizing the research of White (1972), Broderick
(1977), Muir (1977) and Brown (1988), concludes that across the various locales of independent work five common officer styles emerge, which speaks to
the validity and reliability of this line of inquiry. Worden provides a thumbnail sketch of the primary officer styles, identified by typology studies, as they
relate to central aspects of the outlooks and orientations of police culture.

Worden's *tough-cop* approaches police work in a cynical manner, often conflicting with citizens and supervisors in their aggressive approach to selectively
fighting serious crime. Worden explains that these officers do not want to be
bothered with trivial police matters, such as maintaining order or providing
services, and they place a premium on their street experience over formal education. This style of officer would be the stereotypical characterization of the
gruff "cop's cop" in television/movie portrayals—one who is not afraid to push
(or even exceed) the limits of police power if deemed necessary. Interestingly,
the *tough-cop* mirrors monolithic versions of police culture, as well as Reuss-
Ianni's (1983) street cop culture and Manning's (1994) lower participant culture. Worden's (1995) summary of additional styles points to important
cultural segmentation among officers. That is, there are a variety of ways (not
just one) in which officers cope, via their style, with the demands of their occupation.

Worden's *clean-beat crime-fighters* resemble tough-cops in their cynical approach, strong orientations toward crime fighting, and conflicting relationships with supervisors. What separates this style from the former is their
undying pursuit of enforcing all laws, not just the serious ones (in keeping a

clean beat), and their belief that police should follow the procedural rules (i.e., not violate citizen rights). *Avoiders* are described as a cynical group that, as their name implies, avoid as much work as possible. This officer style has a very narrow approach to police work, as they take "laying low" to extremes. Their orientations toward all aspects of the job are rather detached, as they attempt to just do their time.

Problem solvers are those officers with very favorable attitudes toward citizens and the service style of policing. This group is the least oriented toward crime fighting and aggressive policing tactics. As opposed to traditional ways of handling situations, problem solvers focus on outcomes as they like to see problems in their policing areas through to the end. To many traditional police officers, the approaches endorsed by the problem solver would appear as "soft." Finally, *professionals* embody the values of the professional reform movement, and are characterized as the most positive of the five policing styles. Officers in this group hold favorable orientations toward all aspects of their street and organizational environments. Professionals are portrayed as the most well rounded group in terms of performing multiple functions (i.e., broad role orientation) in a manner in which citizens are not treated aggressively, and supervisors approve.

Common Research Methodologies

Like the previous three approaches, those interested in capturing the individual-level nuances of cultural variation among police officers often utilize a combination of research methodologies. Such approaches, which focus predominantly on patrol officers, include structured surveys with Likert-type response categories (e.g., agree strongly, agree somewhat, disagree somewhat, disagree strongly). Often, these are starting points used to categorize or "type" officers based on responses to a variety of attitudinal dimensions reflected in the survey questionnaire. Researchers also assume attitude-behavior congruence or supplement survey methods with unstructured observations with a handful of patrol officers to examine ways in which attitudinal proclivities play out behaviorally on the street. For example, if officers score high on an aggressiveness dimension of an attitudinal survey, do they, in fact, act in an aggressive manner in their dealings with citizens? As part of such observations, researchers also employ open-ended interviews with patrol officers, which serve as narrative accounts of each type. This multi-pronged approach helps solidify researchers' claims regarding an officer's style. Finally, in providing organizational, community, and individual context, researchers (like organizational culture approaches) also rely on a variety of official data.

References

Banton, M. (1964). *The policeman in the community*. London: Tavistock Publications.

Barker, J. C. (1999). *Danger, duty, and disillusion: The worldview of Los Angeles police officers*. Prospect Heights, IL: Waveland Press, Inc.

Bittner, E. (1967). Police on skid row: A Study of peace keeping. *American Sociological Review, 32*, 699–715.

Bittner, E. (1970). *The functions of police in modern society*. Washington, D.C.: U.S. Government Printing Office.

Bittner, E. (1974). Florence Nightingale in pursuit of Willie Sutton: A theory of the police. In H. Jacob (Ed.), *The potential for reform of criminal justice* (pp. 17–44). Beverly Hills, CA: Sage.

Broderick, J. J. (1977). *Police in a time of change*. Morristown, NJ: General Learning Press.

Brown, M. K. (1988). *Working the street: Police discretion and the dilemmas of reform*. New York, NY: Russell Sage Foundation.

Chevigny, P. (1969). *Police power: Police abuses in New York City*. New York, NY: Random House, Inc.

Cochran, J. K., & Bromley, M. L. (2003). The myth(?) of the police sub-culture. *Policing: An International Journal of Police Strategies & Management, 26*, 88–117.

Crank, J. P. (1997). Celebrating agency culture: Engaging a traditional cop's heart in organizational change. In Q. C. Thurman & E. McGarrell (Eds.), *Community policing in a rural setting* (pp. 49–57). Cincinnati, OH: Anderson Publishing Company.

Cullen, F. T., Link, B.G., Travis, L.F. III., & Lemming, T. (1983). Paradoxes in policing: A note on perceptions of danger. *Journal of Police Science and Administration, 11*, 457–462.

Drummond, D. S. (1976). *Police culture*. Beverly Hills, CA: Sage Publications.

Geertz, C. (1973). *The interpretation of cultures: Selected essays*. New York, NY: Basic Books, Inc.

Hassell, K. D. (2007). Variation in police patrol practices: The precinct as a sub-organizational level of analysis. *Policing: An International Journal of Police Strategies & Management, 30*, 257–276.

Herbert, S. (1996). Morality in law enforcement: Chasing 'bad guys' with the Los Angeles Police Department. *Law & Society Review, 30*, 798–818.

Herbert, S. (1998). Police subculture reconsidered. *Criminology, 36*, 343–369.

Jermier, J. M., Slocum, J. W. Jr., Fry, L. W., & Gaines, J. (1991). Organizational subcultures in a soft bureaucracy: Resistance behind the myth and facade of an official culture. *Organizational Science, 2,* 170–194.

Kelling, G. L., & Kliesmet, R. B. (1996). Police unions, police culture, and police abuse of force. In W. A. Geller & H. H. Toch (Eds.), *Police violence* (pp. 191–212). New Haven, CT: Yale University Press.

Klinger, D. A. (1997). Negotiating order in patrol work: An ecological theory of police response to deviance. *Criminology, 35,* 277–306.

Klockars, C. B. (1985). Order maintenance, the quality of urban life, and police: A different line of argument. In W. A. Geller (Ed.), *Police leadership in America: Crisis and opportunity* (pp. 309–321). New York, NY: Praeger.

Louis, M. R. (1983). Organizations as culture-bearing milieu. In L. R. Pondy, P. J. Frost, G. Morgan, and T. C. Dandridge (Eds.), *Organizational Symbolism* (39–54). Greenwich, CT: Jai Press, Inc.

Manning, P. K. (1994). *Police occupational culture: Segmentation, politics, and sentiments.* Unpublished manuscript, Michigan State University.

Manning, P. K. (1995). The police occupational culture in Anglo-American societies. In W. Bailey (Ed.), *The Encyclopedia of Police Science* (pp. 472–475). New York, NY: Garland Publishing Co.

McNamara, J. H. (1967). Uncertainties in police work: The relevance of police recruits' background and training. In D. Bordua (Ed.), *The police: Six sociological essays* (pp. 163–252). New York, NY: John Wiley & Sons.

Merton, R. K. (1938). Social structure and anomie. *American Sociological Review, 3,* 672–682.

Muir, W. K., Jr. (1977). *Police: Streetcorner politicians.* Chicago, IL: University of Chicago Press.

Niederhoffer, A. (1967). *Behind the shield: The police in urban society.* New York, NY: Doubleday.

Paoline, E. A., III. (2001). *Rethinking police culture: Officers' occupational attitudes.* New York, NY: LFB Publishing.

Paoline, E. A., III. (2003). Taking stock: Toward a richer understanding of police culture. *Journal of Criminal Justice, 31,* 199–214.

Paoline, E. A., III. (2004). Shedding light on police culture: An examination of officers' occupational attitudes. *Police Quarterly, 7,* 205–236.

Patton, M. Q. (2002). *Qualitative research & evaluation methods (3rd ed.).* Thousand Oaks, CA: Sage Publications, Inc.

Reuss-Ianni, E. (1983). *Two cultures of policing.* New Brunswick, NJ: Transaction.

Rubinstein, J. (1973). *City police*. New York, NY: Farrar, Straus, and Giroux.

Rumbaut, R. G. & Bittner, E. (1979). Changing conceptions of the police role: A sociological review. In N. Morris & M. Tonry (Eds.), *Crime and justice: An annual review of research* (pp.239–288). Chicago: University of Chicago Press.

Schein, E. H. (1992). *Organizational culture and leadership*. San Francisco, CA: Josey Bass Publishers.

Sellin, T. (1938). *Culture conflict and crime*. New York, NY: Social Science Research Council.

Shaw, C. R., & McKay, H. D. (1942). *Juvenile delinquency in urban areas*. Chicago, IL: University of Chicago Press.

Skolnick, J. H. (1966). *Justice without trial: Law enforcement in democratic society*. New York, NY: John Wiley.

Sparrow, M. K., Moore, M. H., & Kennedy, D. M. (1990). *Beyond 911: A new era for policing*. US: Basic Books Inc.

Toch, H. H. (1973). Psychological consequences of the police role. In E. Eldefonso (Ed.), *Readings in criminal justice* (pp. 85–92). New York, NY: Glencoe Press.

Van Maanen, J. (1974). Working the street: A developmental view of police behavior. In H. Jacob (Ed.), *The potential for reform of criminal justice* (pp. 83–128). Beverly Hills, CA: Sage.

Van Maanen, J. (1978). The asshole. In P. K. Manning & J. Van Maanen (eds.), *Policing: A view from the street* (pp. 221–238). Santa Monica, CA: Goodyear Publishing Company, Inc.

Van Maanen, J. (1984). Making rank: Becoming an American police sergeant. *Urban Life, 13*, 155–176.

Van Maanen, J., & Barley, S. R. (1984). Occupational communities: Culture and control in organizations. In B. M. Staw and C.C. Cummings (Eds.), *Research in organizational behavior* (pp. 287–365). Vol. 6. Greenwich, CT: Jai Press.

Van Maanen, J., & Barley, S. R. (1985). Cultural organization: Fragments of a theory. In P. J. Frost, L. F. Moore, M. R. Louis, C. C. Lundberg, and J. Martin (Eds.). *Organizational culture* (pp. 31–53). Beverly Hills, CA: Sage.

Walker, S., & Katz, C. M. (2008). *The police in America: An introduction (6th ed.)*. New York, NY: McGraw-Hill Companies, Inc.

Westley, W. A. (1970). *Violence and the police: A sociological study of law, custom, and morality*. Cambridge, MA: MIT Press.

White, S. O. (1972). A perspective on police professionalization. *Law & Society Review, 7*, 61–85.

Wilson, J. Q. (1968). *Varieties of police behavior: The management of law and order in eight communities*. Cambridge, MA: Harvard University Press.

Worden, R. E. (1995). Police officers' belief systems: A framework for analysis. *American Journal of Police, 14*, 49–81.

Chapter 2

The Historical Context of Policing: The Evolution of Prevailing Operational Philosophies and the Implications for Police Culture

American policing can generally be divided into several overlapping predominant eras. The earliest, often referred to as the colonial era, began with the initial settlements and lasted through the early- to mid-1800s. The political era, coinciding with the first uniformed or modern policing forces, began in the 1830s and 1840s and lasted until the early- to mid-1900s. The professional era emerged in the early- to mid-1900s and continued throughout much of the remaining century. The community policing era began gaining momentum in the late 1970s and continued into the 21st century. Whether we have entered, or are about to enter, yet another era is to be determined.

In this chapter we examine these various eras by highlighting the main tenets of each, noting key players and their influence, and the broader political and contextual elements occurring at the time (ranging from the role of technology to research). This ultimately leads us to speculate on contemporary changes in the philosophy of policing over the past 10 to 20 years, with a look at the potential death of the once-popular community policing era. As part of this discussion, we will assess how the recent changes in policing mirror past approaches and what we can learn from this history with respect to police culture.

Early American Policing — The Colonial Era

Policing in early America was conducted by a number of different entities such as sheriffs and constables (Walker, 1980). Their role was particularly broad, extending beyond law enforcement or order maintenance duties. For example, sheriffs were often assigned duties such as maintaining roads, collecting taxes, and holding elections. When sheriffs and constables did work within a more traditional crime and justice perspective, it was usually in the form of tracking down and bringing alleged criminals to a magistrate or judge. Relatedly, their job was inherently political and tended to serve local power figures, both politically and economically oriented, rather than the individual citizenry. Not surprisingly, given the lack of an organized police force in any modern sense, everyday citizens were expected to play a large role during this time period. All adult men were expected to serve their community by taking turns conducting a "watch," where they were charged with patrolling the streets looking for fires, crimes, and disorder.

By nearly all historical accounts, the ability to control crime and disorder during this period was severely limited. Patrol was done by foot; communication consisted of in-person contacts; and with the exception of the watch, which at least had a partial proactive element, citizen grievances were handled reactively. Needless to say, the effectiveness of these early forms of social control was severely lacking, and the seeds of corruption and vigilantism were firmly planted within the expanding territories (Lane, 1967).

Police Culture in the Colonial Era

In considering police culture during this era, the cohesion that bound officers to one another was more a function of community homogeneity, among those with whom they chose to reside, over any distinct features of the volunteer service for which they were performing. Such cultural homogeneity would become more formalized during the next era, as the volunteer nature of policing transformed to a full-time paid occupation.

19th Century Policing — The Political Era

America's population in the early 19th century nearly doubled, increasing from just over five million people in 1800 to nearly 10 million by 1820 (U.S. Census Bureau). With such rapid population gain came growing crime and disorder problems, along with industrialization, poverty, immigrant clashes, and at times riots. As public concern grew in urban centers such as Boston, New York, and Philadelphia, city leaders struggled with how best to maintain order, while not infringing on the early American spirit of freedom and individual rights. Local politicians and community members were forced to begin discussing the need for a more organized system of controlling crime and disorder. Yet, it would be years before any serious type of organized policing would take hold. Citizens were fearful of any form of national police agency. Partisan political fights for control at the state and local levels became commonplace. And, citizens were not overly enthusiastic about the prospects of paying taxes for a more organized system of policing (Walker, 1977).

Meanwhile, England was facing many of the same issues, and a number of parliamentary committees were tasked with investigating the best options for controlling disorder. This ultimately led to the first Metropolitan Police Act, which formally established the Metropolitan Police Force in 1829 (London Metropolitan Police, 2013). Robert Peel, serving as the Home Secretary at the time, is widely credited as the father of modern day policing, but both Richard Mayne and Charles Rowan were also vital in shaping the new style of policing that would emerge in the coming years. This style would ultimately include several important elements: (1) a semi or quasi-military hierarchal organizational structure consisting of divisions and companies, and staffed by uniformed superintendents, inspectors, sergeants, and constables; (2) a preventative patrol strategy whereby officers would police the streets on foot in fixed beats; and (3) an overarching organizational mission centered on crime prevention first, as opposed to simply responding to crime after the fact. Although this new organization initially faced challenges such as garnering public acceptance and leading to appropriate officer behavior (e.g., in the first six months alone over half of the roughly 3,000 officers were fired, often for drunkenness), this style of policing would eventually set the standard for modernized policing (Miller, 1977).

Following England's lead, organized police forces in major American cities began to take shape in the 1830s and 1840s amid continued political, economic, and cultural conflicts. The English approach was influential not only in terms of organizational structure, patrol strategy, and mission, but also with respect to the importance of local control, thus leading to tremendous fragmentation but on a grander scale. Nonetheless, while the English model became widely respected for demonstrating the use of restraint in forceful tactics, high personnel standards, and strict supervision, the American model went in the opposite direction. Uniformed officers, similar to their earlier sheriff and constable counterparts, were heavy-handed when it came to the use of force; and personnel standards and supervision were essentially nonexistent, as the political patronage system took control of hiring, promoting, and dismissing officers (Miller, 1977).

Overall, police work in the U.S. throughout much of the 19th century can be characterized as ineffective, inefficient, brutal, and corrupt (Walker, 1977). Police officers predominately patrolled their beats on foot. Communication was mainly by word of mouth. Even after call boxes were introduced in the latter portion of the century, they were of limited use as the technology of the day was inherently deficient. Police work was almost exclusively reactive in nature, and supervision of officers was nearly impossible. As the population continued to increase, the police were expected to take on more and more of an expanded social role, such as operating homeless shelters out of precinct houses (Monkkonen, 1992). There were simply no other established governmental agencies designed to handle society's growing problems. In many jurisdictions there was a never-ending battle for who would control the police, as the political patronage system became well entrenched. Police officers were selected based on political affiliation as opposed to skill sets. There were no personnel or training standards. Officers were provided a badge and baton and instructed to hit the street, often for the purpose of enhancing the controlling party's vested labor and economic interests. Thus, corruption and brutality were commonplace and the public's image of the police was unflattering at best, setting the stage for the "keystone kops" moniker depicted in the silent films of the early 1900s (Haller, 1976; Lane, 1967).

Police Culture in the Political Era

During this time period, conditions of the primary work environments started to take shape but did not become fully crystalized until the next period. For example, working large geographic areas alone contributed to much of the heavy-handed nature of performing patrol arrest functions (especially among drunk and disorderly citizens). The reciprocal violence between corrupt officers who were brutalizing citizens (in ethnically homogenous areas), and citizens who were fighting back to avoid arrest for themselves (or family members and countrymen), drove a wedge in the relationship between the police and the public. At the same time, the "cat and mouse" game between patrol officers and their supervisors began to define organizational mechanisms of laying low. Like the previous era, the police were a relatively culturally homogenous occupational group, but such cohesion was now less a function of where they resided and more formalized in the sense that it was based on their political connections. Such connections were responsible for gaining (and ensuring continued) police employment, and were also tied to one's ethnicity.

As a result, police forces, at this point in time, were ethnically, politically, and culturally similar.

20th Century Policing Part I— The Professional Era

As the 20th century began, a broad-based movement that became known as the "Progressive Era" took form. With Theodore Roosevelt helping lead the way, followers of this movement, proudly referred to as progressives, sought political, economic, and social reform designed to improve the lives of every-day common citizens, not just the leaders of industry and government. Progressives pushed for increased regulation of large corporations and improved working conditions (e.g., eight-hour work days). They promoted social justice for the poor, needy, and disenfranchised (e.g., women's suffrage). They called for improved governmental efficiency through centralized decision making and direct control (e.g., a city-manager system) (Gould, 2001).

It was within this progressive framework that early police reformers began to emerge with similar ideals. Richard Sylvester served as Superintendent of the Washington, DC police and President of the International Association of Chiefs of Police (IACP), thereby lending a national voice to police reform. August Vollmer was Chief of Police in Berkeley (California), author of the 1931 Wickersham Commission report on the police, and long-time advocate for higher education. Vollmer's student, Orlando Winfield Wilson (better known as OW), went on to become Superintendent of the Chicago Police Department and co-author of perhaps the most influential textbook (Police Administration, 1950) in the history of policing; although some may argue that Raymond Fosdick's *American Police Systems*, published in 1920, was also highly influential in the early days of the professional policing era. At the federal level, J. Edgar Hoover (FBI Director) became the face of the movement.

The overarching theme of police reformers during this era was to make policing a "profession." Theoretically, professionalization would mirror that of such occupations as law, medicine, and education, which would involve extensive levels of training, education, and supervised experience prior to plying one's craft alone in the field. The ideal in this style of professionalism would not require an extensive use of policies, procedures, or a rigid set of rules. Rather, the skilled practitioner would be given great latitude and autonomous decision making. Interestingly, however, the form of police professionalism that would take hold did not necessarily take a similar format in this regard. In fact, while everyday police decision making by patrol officers would continue to involve much discretion, policing took on enormous bureaucratic structural features in the name of professionalism (Walker, 1977).

The professional model of policing was guided by several tenets. One of the key elements was to address the influence of politics. The political model of policing came to be known as the political model for a reason—because of the extent to which politics were embedded within the institution from top to bottom (Lane, 1967). Professional model advocates wanted police administrators to manage their organizations separate and apart from local political influence to the greatest extent possible, under the belief that the police should not be used as the coercive arm of political interests (whether legitimate or illegitimate). Moreover, police leaders employed an organizational philosophy designed to fight crime and control disorder, not engage in corrupt behavior for the purpose of further lining ones' own pockets.

Another mainstay of the professionalization movement was an emphasis placed on scientific management and classic organizational theory. A large part of this approach involved moving to a more centralized and hierarchical command structure (i.e., top-down decision making). Under the political model, decentralization was a mainstay. However, professional model reformers called for a more stringent hierarchal structure, which involved closing decentralized precincts in many larger cities and having employees report out of a central location. The belief was that such a system would yield a stronger chain of command and less corruption.

There was also great emphasis placed on the use of written rules and standard operating procedures (SOPs), general supervision, discipline, and tighter control of the rank and file. For the first time police leaders started to push for objective recruitment practices involving minimum standards to become a police officer, that would be objectively based as opposed to politically based. In this sense, police officers would be selected based on what they knew rather than who they knew. Another tenet focused on pre-service training and the development of police training academies. Officers were to be properly trained prior to hitting the streets with firearm in hand.

Specialization also played a large role under the professional model. First, the police role would be significantly narrowed. Professional model advocates played up the role of crime fighter, while downplaying order maintenance functions. Emphasis was placed on serious crime and arrest rates. Second, the introduction of specialized units such as homicide, robbery, and vice became central features of the professional model. This further fed into the crime fighter image and before long police officers widely eschewed any reference to policing being "social work." Police officers were to be tough, straight laced, crew-cut wearing, crime fighting machines ready to show up on time, follow departmental orders, and catch the bad guys. Arrests for homicide, robbery, and rape were highly valued, while engaging in low level peacekeeping activities was not.

Somewhat interestingly, professional model leaders such a Sylvester, Vollmer, and Wilson paid little attention to the primary actors within a police department—line-level officers (i.e., patrol officers). Rather, they choose instead to focus primarily on management and leadership. Such a decision did not go unrecognized by those who did the everyday heavy lifting and helped plant the early *loyalty* seeds of the police culture and eventual unionization. This development was also somewhat ironic given that the professional model was rooted within the broader progressive movement that championed the rights of everyday workers.

Importantly, the confluence of several technological advances (telephone, two-way radio, and patrol car) during the 20th century helped propel professional-style policing. At a minimum, when citizens witnessed a crime or wanted to report one, they could use the telephone to call the police, the dispatcher could then radio an officer in a patrol car, who could then respond to the scene quickly. Moreover, the predominant policing strategy became three fold (i.e., random preventative patrol, fast response, criminal investigation). First, police officers were able to engage in random preventative patrol seeking to deter potential offenders from committing a crime in the first place. The general belief being that patrolling would allow officers to be anywhere at anytime so would-be criminals be forewarned (i.e., the notion of the police being an omnipresence). Second, if patrol officers were unable to prevent a crime through their random patrols, then they would be in a position to respond quickly to a call if a crime occurred. The belief being that a fast response would lead to a greater probability of the suspect still being on the scene and subsequently apprehended by the efficient officer. If both of these measures failed (the prevention of a crime or on-scene arrest), specialized investigative units would be available to follow up and make an arrest. The belief was that detective work was contingent on highly skilled investigators able to close cases patrol officers could not.

By the 1960s, the traditional model was firmly established in many police agencies. However, it was during this time period that policing as a collective whole also began to face scrutiny. First, a series of landmark Supreme Court cases (*Mapp v. Ohio*, 1961; *Escobedo v. Illinois*, 1964; *Miranda v. Arizona*, 1966) started to raise concern over police practices. Second, a number of aggressive police-citizen encounters sparked major riots in cities across the country (e.g., Detroit, Los Angeles, Newark). A divide was becoming increasingly apparent between the police and the community they were supposed to serve, especially within the context of racial relations. Early police scholars such as Skolnick (1969) and Westley (1970) were writing about the manner in which the police viewed the public and vice versa. Popular phrases common today such as "us versus them" and the "code" or "blue wall of silence" were gaining traction. In short, some communities were questioning whether the police were becoming too distant from the public, thereby creating an adversarial relationship. Questions began to emerge such as: Is the narrowly defined police role (i.e., that of a crime fighter) now a detriment in terms of establishing any rapport or connection with the public?

With these legal, civil rights, and social justice issues as a backdrop, the federal government formed the Law Enforcement Assistance Administration (LEAA) in 1968 as a means to improve police practice through the use of federal funds distributed to local and state agencies. Police researchers and practitioners finally started to ask seemingly long overdue questions such as: Does random preventive patrol prevent crime? Does rapid response increase the probability of arrest? Do highly skilled criminal investigators matter in terms of solving a crime? The results of studies examining these questions in the 1970s were not overly encouraging (see Greenwood & Petersilia, 1975; Kelling et al., 1974; Spelman & Brown, 1984). Although wrought with a series of methodological limitations (see Sherman, 2013), there was little evidence presented that preventative random patrol, rapid response, or criminal investigation were very effective, thus calling into question the unholy trinity upon which the primary policing strategies of the entire professional model rested.

Police Culture in the Professional Era

The professional era represents a critical period for police culture, even as we know it today. During this time, the organizational environment became formalized, with some very specific reform recommendations. The bureaucratization of American police agencies, which called for tighter administrative control and supervision of officers, worked to further forge a gap between the policing ranks than the "cat and mouse" avoidance procedures noted in the previous era. As such, supervisors concerned themselves with incorporating the various tenets of the professional reform (i.e., either at the top level in structuring change or in the middle in executing the plan), while the day-to-day operations of keeping the streets crime free fell on the shoulders of patrol officers. Such a division became exacerbated in the 1960s when the U.S. Supreme Court placed "restrictions" on officers' crime fighting abilities, as supervisors were now responsible for making sure their subordinates followed the procedural rules, regardless of the substantive outcomes. Laying low from such scrutiny by supervisors and trusting only one's peers (loyalty) became prominent cultural dimensions during this period. At the same time, the bureaucratization of police agencies (and the strains placed on officers) was not being equally distributed across departments, as community composition and political structure represented sources of variation in organizational approaches/styles (Wilson, 1968).

From an occupational environment perspective, the streets were still characterized as dangerous and hostile, as officers were exerting their coercive control over citizens in their aggressive pursuit of fighting crime. The division between the police and the public, noted in the previous era, became more amplified (especially in minority communities), as several of the tenets of the professional reform (e.g., replacing foot with automobile patrol, aggressive crime fighting tactics, "just the facts ma'am" approaches to citizen engagement, etc.) for the first time received criticism from national review commissions (Walker, 1977).

Cumulatively, the 20th century reform was helping shape the occupational culture of police. At the same time, despite criticisms regarding unintended consequences (i.e., in terms of police-citizen relations), the reform was deemed to be more positive than negative. This prompted scholarly work (i.e., typologies) into the extent to which patrol officers embodied the primary values of professionalization (White, 1972).

Finally, we witnessed the beginning of vast changes in the demographic characteristics of police officers. The Kerner Commission, charged with examining police-community relations following a series of highly publicized riots in the late 1960s, recommended that American police agencies hire more minority officers as a way to improve the hostile relationship between the police and the public (Walker, 1977). In addition, the 1964 Civil Rights Act, and the subsequent Equal Employment Opportunity Act of 1972, led to increases in the number of women being hired for street-level patrol positions across American police agencies (Martin, 1997). Finally, the 1967 President's Commission on Law Enforcement and the Administration of Justice called for the college education of line officers, as opposed to the reformers' recommendation for just the police leaders (Paoline & Terrill, 2007). These efforts were supplemented with federal monies (i.e., Law Enforcement Education Program-LEEP), which resulted in increased numbers of patrol officers with college experience and degrees (Eskridge, 1989). Overall, the demographic homogeneity of police officers (i.e., White, males, high school educated) started to change during the end of this era.

The professional era, perhaps the period that witnessed more changes in policing than any other, not coincidently was also when several shared cultural features emerged. At the same time, there were a number of mechanisms of cultural fragmentation operating, based on rank, organizational style, officer style, and officer composition. The latter portion of this century, as detailed in the next section, introduced a significant philosophical change with important implications for police culture.

20th Century Policing Part II — The Community Policing Era

Community policing saw its roots beginning to grow in the late 1970s and into the early 1980s. Yet, defining this philosophy of policing with any degree of precision was, and some might say still is, elusive. Nonetheless, much like the professional model which contained several central elements, community policing entailed numerous tenets or basic principles. Advocates of this model of policing sought to redefine the police role within a broader context. Part of this movement centered on looking beyond individuals and toward neighborhood-level disorder as a collective whole. Another part of this broadening involved explicitly recognizing that policing is about much more than just the law enforcement function (i.e., crime fighting and arrests), which the professional model idealized. As stated by Mastrofski, Worden, and Snipes (1995: p. 541):

> There is no consensus on what community policing is, but one has emerged regarding what it is not. It rejects law enforcement as the single, core function of police. Arrest is only a means to other ends, whether it is maintaining order, improving the quality of neighborhood life, or solving an array of social problems. It holds that there are times when, despite the technical requirements of the law, arrest is not the best choice.

In addition to expanding the police role beyond the law enforcement function, community policing called for enhanced problem-solving rather than simply responding to calls for service, handling the issue as rapidly as possible (via use of the arrest function), and then getting back into service ready to take another call. Relatedly, there was an increasing recognition that the public and the police should work together to prevent and control crime (i.e., the police should develop closer ties with citizens). Advocates called for police agencies to incorporate more bike and foot patrols, and to set up mini-stations to better serve this relationship. While patrol officers and citizens were generally given low priority during the professional era, it was clear that both actors took center stage within a community policing framework. Moreover, the police should go a step further by also engaging with other governmental agencies as well as private industry. The belief being that multiple groups were more capable of solving problems than police alone.

A series of distinct organizational changes was also part of the community policing movement. Geographic responsibility became an important dimension, which called for police officers to be assigned to fixed beats for a consistent amount of time (usually at least a year). Such a development was in direct contrast to basic operations within a professional model design, whereby rotating beats was common practice for fear of corruption, via the police and public becoming too close. Community policing took the opposite stance. The thought process was that the benefits of developing a close police-citizen relationship outweighed the fear of officers engaging in corrupt behavior, especially since the professional model era brought with it the basic practice of objective recruitment and training.

Decentralization of command was also a key part of community policing, which was also in direct opposition to the approach employed under the professional model. Community policing advocates argued that not only should individual officers be given greater discretion, but precinct and district commanders should as well. The underlying belief system was that different parts of a city often faced different types of problems (e.g., the central business ward encounters different types of crime than residential neighborhoods), and thus commanders should have the flexibility to respond differently to such.

Finally, information management started to become more widely used within police agencies during this era. The patrol car, telephone, and two-way radio stimulated change during the professional model. Now, the growing use of computers and a greater appreciation for how data could be collected, stored, and used within an operational framework (not just administrative), started to impact policing. In particular, by the 1990s research on "hot spots" started to gain notice within the field, and police agencies were interested in how to reallocate officers away from random preventative patrol.

With these basic principles serving as a backdrop, and federal support coming from monetary funds ($9 billion) established in the 1994 Violent Crime Control and Law Enforcement Act (i.e., Crime Act), police agencies began implementing various forms of community policing by picking and choosing to emphasize some basic tenets more than others. By the end of the century it was fairly clear that three predominant styles of community policing had taken hold.

One style of community policing, perhaps best described as "community organizing," centered on the police-citizen relationship (i.e., building partnerships) as its defining feature. With the assistance of long-time scholar Wesley Skogan, the Chicago (IL) Police Department (i.e., the Chicago Alternative

Policing Strategy or CAPS) implemented this form of community policing in the early 1990s. The main focus was on increasing police-citizen interactions through the use of neighborhood level/beat meetings. Permanent beat assignments, inter-governmental involvement, crime mapping, and various forms of problem-solving, also became staples of the CAPS approach. What helped make Chicago even more interesting to agencies around the country was the decision to go citywide with CAPS, rather than having a specialized community policing unit separate and apart from a general patrol unit. That is, all patrol officers (with some exceptions for rapid response) were expected to be community policing officers.

A second form of community policing that took shape, popularized by Herman Goldstein (1979), was "Problem-Oriented Policing" or POP. Goldstein felt that the police, through years of socialization under a professional model ideology, were overly concerned with the means of policing (e.g., quickly responding to calls, staffing and management issues) over the ends (i.e., solving the problem). First implemented in smaller U.S. cities such as Newport News (VA) and Madison (WI), and later in larger cities such as St. Petersburg (FL) and San Diego (CA), the basic premise called for patrol officers to think about underlying causes of recurring problems, rather than simply continue to respond to call after call as if they were isolated incidents. What helped propel this style of policing was the eventual development of a planning template called SARA, which stood for Scanning, Analysis, Response, and Assessment (Eck & Spelman, 1987; Goldstein, 1990). SARA would allow everyday patrol officers to consider all the potential problems in their given beat (i.e., Scanning); gather information to determine the extent, nature, and potential cause of problems (i.e., Analysis); develop and implement solutions to underlying problems (i.e., Response); and then to assess whether the response was effective (i.e., Assessment). Goldstein (1990) recognized that the use of an arrest, which is offender based, was not necessarily the easiest or best way to solve problems, and encouraged officers to think how victims or environmental features might be altered instead (i.e., thinking through the entire crime triangle of offenders, victims, and place).

A third predominant model that developed during the community policing era emanated from James Q. Wilson and George Kelling's "broken windows" article published in 1982. In this theoretical piece, the authors describe how social disorder and physical decay facilitate crime at the neighborhood level. Such a process begins when a community and the police fail to address lower level quality of life issues (e.g., loitering, drinking in public, vandalism, graffiti, abandoned houses), because such problems create fear of crime and neighborhood decay. Used as a metaphor, they argue broken windows that are not repaired are a sign that no one cares and encourage other neighborhood residents to neglect their property. This then sets in motion a downward spiral of deterioration. Houses and buildings become dilapidated, homeowners move out as property values decrease, more rental properties take over, which increases transiency. Those left behind become scared to go out into the neighborhood so they shut themselves in and withdraw from getting involved, further weakening the informal social control network. As all this occurs, the disorderly element begins to take control of the neighborhood, and more serious crime sets in.

From an operational standpoint, Wilson and Kelling (1982) argue that the problem with traditional (i.e., professional model) policing is that it focused on the "end" result of this process: serious crime. When crimes such a homicide, robbery, and aggravated assault become embedded within a community, the police have but a limited capacity to control it. As a result, the police need to intervene early in the process by cracking down on social and physical level disorder. Use of the arrest function under this style of community policing is very much valued, although not necessarily required. Over the years broken windows policing has also been labeled aggressive order maintenance policing, as well as zero-tolerance policing (rightly or wrongly). In the 1990s, under the direction of then Mayor Rudolph Giuliani, the New York Police Department (NYPD) implemented broken windows style policing, bringing with it full scale national exposure.

In terms of whether community policing works, research findings to date are rather varied. First, there is no question there was been great hype surrounding community policing, and most police executives claim they engaged in it. Upon closer inspection, however, the entire community policing movement was probably (and may still be) much more rhetoric than reality, in terms of the extent to which police agencies actually altered their organizational systems and resulting actions (see Greene, 2004; Roth, Roehl, & Johnson, 2004). As stated by Dabney (2010: p. 30), "Where community policing is concerned, it is generally agreed that the posturing far outweighed the practical outcomes." That is, there is little evidence to suggest that community policing was ever fully incorporated or implemented in most police agencies beyond a few token gestures (e.g., some foot patrol, a few officers assigned to community duties, bike patrol limited to the central business district) due the enormous difficulty of trying to reorganize and establish service delivery that strays from traditional crime fighting. Even in agencies nationally recognized as community policing leaders, upon looking beneath the surface the limitations of implementation were often seen. In just one example, the St. Petersburg (FL) Police Department, which was widely regarded at the forefront of the movement in the mid-1990s, had just nine percent of its officers (48 of 520) assigned to community policing duties. The remaining 91 percent functioned in a traditional style of policing, geared toward the crime fighting function.

Although community policing was not necessarily as fully entrenched as the public may have been led to believe, there were enough departments engaged in the practice for researchers to be able to assess effectiveness over the years. So what's the verdict? Does it work? The answer seems to depend more upon the style of community policing. Perhaps the most evidence can be found for problem-oriented policing. In conducting a systematic review, Weisburd and colleagues (2010: p. 140), while recognizing some limitations, concluded "an overwhelmingly positive impact from POP." Evidence of effectiveness for the community organizing and broken windows models are more mixed. For instance, Skogan and Steiner (2004) offered a series of grades when assessing the CAPS model. They gave an "A" to Chicago's efforts at agency partnerships and reorganization, a "B" to public involvement, and a "C" to the department's efforts at problem-solving. Finally, assessing the impact of broken windows policing has presented a series of conceptual and methodical challenges with the evidence difficult to determine at this stage (see Braga & Bond, 2008; Chappell, Monk-Turner, & Payne, 2011).

Police Culture in the Community Policing Era

The philosophical changes in policing, as part of community policing efforts, offered several opportunities for segmentation in the occupational police culture, as officers (in varying degrees) were operating in altered work environments. On the street, community policing initiatives encouraged patrol officers to establish long-term, collaborative (with citizens) investments in their assigned areas. This provided a patrol environment where there could be reduced levels of danger and hostility, less of a focus on coercive tactics, decreased suspicion and distrust of citizens, and less isolation between the police and the public. Operationally, this was undoing many of the shortcomings of the professional era (i.e., separating the police from the public and failure to substantially reduce crime), and resembled the approaches of the political era (i.e., officers walking the beat and closely connected to citizens), without the corruption.

The organizational environment was also altered, as departments were hierarchically flattened and decentralized (like the political era), with recommendations for supervisors to grant subordinates discretionary freedom to come up with "outside the box" solutions to neighborhood-level problems and disorders. In addition, supervisors were also to encourage, and provide reward incentives for, subordinates to embrace a broader role orientation beyond the strict crime control mandates espoused during the prior era. This transformed environment provided opportunities for officers to rely less on laying low/CYA approaches to deal with supervisory scrutiny and also worked to expand their role to include order maintenance and community policing functions. The fewer bureaucratic layers, as part of flattening the police hierarchy, also provided mechanisms for officers to break down divisions with other units and ranks that had built up for over half a century.

While federal monies were provided during this era that ensured that virtually no department would refuse to incorporate some component(s) of the various community policing approaches, street-level officers, on the other hand, did not equally embrace this change in policing philosophy (Paoline, Myers, & Worden, 2000). As such, the traditional occupational culture that was built in the prior era, while perhaps less popular in the community era, was not dead. Officers could still embrace such tenets, although there were alternative cultural options available (i.e., for those endorsing the new philosophy and/or those specifically assigned to this specialization). This, coupled with the continued recruitment and selection of demographically diverse personnel, which started at the end of the preceding era, provided the potential for a less culturally homogenous (i.e., fragmented) occupational group.

21st Century Policing—Post 9/11 Policing

Unlike our review of earlier policing eras, not enough time has elapsed within the present period to offer a systematic breakdown of what 21st century policing will ultimately look like. Nonetheless, we can offer a description of the major practices that seem to be driving the policing enterprise as of 2013. Of course, the 9/11 attacks have already played a key role in reshaping policy at the national level. With the establishment of the Department of Homeland Security (DHS), one of the largest reorganizations of the federal government in the past half century occurred. In total, 22 federal agencies and departments came under the umbrella of the DHS. State and local agencies have a role in counter-terrorism, and at times a rather large role during crisis management events (as was witnessed after the Boston Marathon Bombings in 2013), but such a role will inherently remain somewhat limited for two primary reasons. First, while there is little disagreement that local police are important from an "eyes and ears" or "look, listen, report" or "information gathering" perspective, the federal authorities steer the ship both in terms of information analyses and larger operational response.

Second, the heart of everyday policing remains. That is, all order maintenance activities, and all but national security related crime fighting activities, remain at the local level. It is the local cop who is still charged with
responding to everyday reports ranging from disabled vehicles blocking traffic, to lost children, to noise complaints, to neighbor disputes, to burglaries,
to homicides. Hence, at its core, policing at the municipal level for the patrol officer may be forever changed to some degree post 9/11, but the extent
of such change will be limited given the American fragmented system of local
control.

Additionally, racial tensions are still very much part of the policing enterprise, as is the ever delicate nature of police use of force and the balanc-
ing act of constantly assessing the dual role of the police in terms of protecting
the general citizenry while also preserving individual rights. Of course, as of
2013, neither of these issues is on the same scale in comparison to earlier
eras. Finally, the economic crisis of 2008 is still impacting police budgets
across the country as agencies try to do more with less, and police consoli-
dation (and in drastic cases, agency disbandment) is becoming a reality in
some areas.

What follows is a brief review of emerging policing strategies, some of which
have been in operation for 20 years now and demonstrate promise in terms of
successful implementation and positive outcomes. Others presently appear to
contain more hype or rhetoric, to borrow from earlier community policing day
lingo, than actual substance, but at least offer potential. Prior to discussing more
specific strategies, however, it is worth noting the nature of "evidence-based"
policing, an underlying feature of many of the approaches outlined below. Evidence-based is certainly a popular phrase in contemporary terms, and one that
policing scholars clearly like, for it has easy-to-follow logic that crime control
policy and practice should be based on *science*. The romanticized version of evidence-based practice is often linked to the medical field, whereby science drives
practice (Sherman, 1998). Despite the fact that there is little evidence that such
always occurs, this has not stopped policing scholars from pushing evidence-
based practice. The idea is clearly sound. Who would argue against the police
acting in ways that have been shown to prevent and control crime or disorder?
Sure, the police should engage in what works and what has been shown to be
effective policing. Yet, there are at least three potential difficulties that may hin-
der such science-based practice moving forward.

First, as the medical field has demonstrated, there is often a significant gap
between researchers and practitioners. While both parties may talk a good
game, and banter about the importance of science at professional conferences
and in academic journals, the scores of everyday practitioners who are in the

field at the ground level often pay little attention, let alone seek to implement such field research. Your everyday primary care physician, much like your everyday patrol officer, is primarily oriented toward handling daily tasks with little time or inclination to determine what the researchers are doing. Additionally, "experience" matters to point of contact service providers, often much more than what is printed in a journal.

Second, even if police managers and street-level officers take time to educate themselves on the latest science, it would have to be deemed of sufficient quality and it would require effort. Our experience to date is that "quality" research in the eyes of many police officers is something read in trade magazines such as the *Police Chief* or *FBI Bulletin*. The concept of full (or perhaps blind or objective) peer review is often lost. Of course, the blame is often put on academic scholars, because their work in traditional peer-review journals (e.g., *Criminology*, *Justice Quarterly*, *Police Quarterly*) is filled with "academic jargon" and difficult to follow "statistical language and formulas." Fair enough, but moving forward in an evidence-based world requires effort not only by scholars who produce the science, but also from practitioners who are expected to consume the science. For example, despite countless protests the authors have heard over the years from former and current students, theory and statistics do matter, and they can only be diluted (for consumption) so much. As a result, policing students need to view and study such topics seriously, not see them solely as a burden to bear and courses to simply cross off their graduation checklist.

Third, policing is a field rich in historical reminiscing and long honored traditions. The glory days of policing. The good old days when cops could be cops. The days when suspects could be treated as suspects rather than coddled like babies; or even when suspects could be called suspects and not persons of interest. When good cops were those with a feel and gut for the job, or a father or uncle who taught them the importance of loyalty and disciple, not those with a fancy college degree or who believe that the voice is more important than the stick. When the community was there to serve and work at the bequest of the police, not on equal footing with them. In short, the police believe they are a special breed. They run toward the exploding building not away from it. They are the thin blue line, which makes them unique, and more importantly, to be placed on higher ground, especially within the context of blue-collar upbringing principles. Furthermore, many cops want to chase and catch the bad guy, clear and simple. And, while the catching part is certainly important, they very much enjoy the chasing part and the *esprit de corps* that is often accompanied by such. How evidence-based policing fits into this viewpoint (albeit not one necessarily always accurate) remains to be seen. While in some instances there may be a good fit (e.g., better information sharing leading to the identification and arrest of a suspect), in other instances perhaps not so much (e.g., better information sharing leading to the identification and arrest of suspects—from the [dis]comfort of sitting in front a computer terminal).

Within this context we turn to those policing strategies that have received considerable attention over the past 20-plus years and appear to be fundamental elements of contemporary policing, or hope to be moving forward. One should not assume the programs listed below are exhaustive, but rather illustrative of the most popular presently. Certainly, additional worthy strategies (e.g., third-party policing) are also being applied at any given time in various agencies.

Hot Spots Policing

In the late 1980s, researchers conducted the "Minneapolis Hot Spots Experiment." One of the key findings coming from this study was that just three percent of city addresses produced 50 percent of all calls for police service over the course of one year. Additionally, 60 percent of city addresses had no calls for service (Sherman, Gartin, & Buerger, 1989). Prior to the Minneapolis study, most scholars were generally more interested in crime from a larger geographic perspective, usually at the neighborhood level. The extent to which crime clustered at distinct addresses in Minneapolis was particularly enlightening, and helped kick start a policing strategy commonly known today as hot spots policing.

A crime hot spot, according to Eck and colleagues (2005: p. 2) "is an area that has a greater than average number of criminal or disorder events, or an area where people have a higher than average risk of victimization." An important consideration, however, is geographic size. Hot spots are generally no larger than one street block and often smaller (e.g., a bar, parking lot, single building, street corner). More directly, the Bureau of Justice Assistance (2013) notes that hot spots are "very small, discrete areas such as blocks, streets, intersections, clusters of addresses and sometimes even individual addresses."

Recall that one of the primary policing strategies of the professional era was random preventative patrol. However, such patrol was designed at the beat or neighborhood level, an area much larger than the notion of contemporary hot spots. In terms of hot spots policing then, the idea is to concentrate resources in small select locations. That is, instead of officers randomly driving around their beats, officers should focus on known trouble spots. Of course, the first step in this process is to identify such hot spots.

The use of computer technology and crime mapping has played a large role in this respect. As of 2007, roughly 75 percent of all police officers in the United States worked for an agency using computerized crime mapping (Reaves, 2010).

Once hot spots are identified, police agencies must then decide how to go about policing these areas. One such tactic is the use of directed patrol, whereby officers are deployed to these small locations to simply create a very visible deterrent threat, to engage in crackdowns (i.e., high levels of enforcement), and/or take a problem-oriented policing approach. As noted by Braga, Papachristos, & Hureau (2012), the extent to which police agencies have latched on to this form of policing is widespread. More specifically, they note that the "nearly 9 out of 10 agencies used hot spots policing strategies to deal with violent crime in their jurisdictions and that problem-solving techniques were often deployed to address violent crime hot spots" (p. 7).

In a time of economic distress, the ability to more finely deploy resources can be tremendously beneficial, especially if patrol officers are reassigned from areas with little or no calls for service to hot spots locations. In such a scenario, a department would have an even greater visible presence (and crackdown and POP capabilities). As found in the Minneapolis study, 60 percent of city addresses had no calls for service. Hence, pulling officers from these locations would seem beneficial. However, from a community perspective (or community policing angle), citizens living in such areas may resist this type of redeployment, irrespective of the crime benefits that may be gleaned in the areas most afflicted. Another concern often raised by police officials, especially street-level patrol officers, is the fear of crime displacement (i.e., crime moving from one geographic hot spot to surrounding locations). Nonetheless, the evidence on hot spots policing is generally strong not only in terms of both crime control and displacement, but also with respect to crime diffusion (i.e., a reduction in crime in surrounding locations). In a recent Campbell Systematic review on hot spots policing, Braga and colleagues (2012: p. 6) conclude: "The extant evaluation research provides fairly robust evidence that hot spots policing is an effective crime prevention strategy. The research also suggests that focusing police efforts on high-activity crime places does not inevitably lead to crime displacement, and crime control benefits may diffuse into the areas immediately surrounding the targeted locations."

Compstat

Compstat, standing for compare statistics, was popularized by the New York City Police Department in the early- to mid-1990s. As the name suggests, the use of statistics was a central feature of this model, within the context of both identifying crime patterns (via computerized crime analysis and mapping) and tracking what is being done to address such crime (via management and accountability mechanisms). As stated by Dabney (2010: p. 28), Compstat consists of "a strategic management model of policing wherein: (1) departmental objectives and resources are focused on a clearly defined set of organizational objectives; (2) police operations are guided by four core management principles (gathering accurate and timely intelligence, designing effective strategies and tactics, the rapid deployment of personnel and resources, and relentless follow-up and assessment); and (3) command decision-making is decentralized into geographic districts."

In New York during the 1990s, the primary objective and key strategy became controlling crime through the use of aggressive order maintenance tactics on quality-of-life offenses (in line with the "Broken Windows" thesis outlined by Wilson & Kelling, 1982). Organizationally, the command structure was reorganized into a more streamlined (i.e., flatter) system of control that called for geographic responsibility at the precinct level. Theoretically, this form of command control would then continue down the supervisory chain to platoon commanders, onward to first-line supervisors (i.e., sergeants), and ultimately to street-level patrol officers. Within each precinct the expectation was that officials would use timely or "real time" data, drawn from a variety of sources (e.g., calls for service, reported crime, arrest), to identify problem areas and people (e.g., hot spots, repeat offenders). Commanders and officers would then institute a game plan for attacking the targeted problem in a timely manner (e.g., enhanced visibility, increased arrests, the use of civil code enforcement). The final component involved follow-up assessment and accountability through regular Compstat meetings. During these meetings top police officials would call in precinct commanders to inquire (or some might say interrogate) whether the commanders were sufficiently aware of the main problems in their area, to determine what was being done about such problems, and to assess whether the strategies being used were working. Failure to solve or reduce identified problems could lead to commanders being sanctioned or demoted.

By the beginning of the year 2000, over half of all police agencies with 100 or more sworn officers in the United States had adopted (one-third) or planned to adopt (one-fourth) some version of Compstat (Weisburd et al., 2003). As of 2013, the Compstat model still appears to be quite popular with law enforcement agencies across the country. However, the extent to which Compstat has been successfully implemented in other jurisdictions beyond New York City, serves as an effective managerial accountability system, or results in reducing crime and disorder is open to debate. For example, according to Dabney (2010: p. 32), "there remains a taken-for-grantedness about the way that the implementation of the structures and processes of this new management model interface with everyday realities of rank-and-file officers working in a metropolitan police department." Others note that Compstat appears to be used as a reinforcing mechanism for more traditional aspects of policing (e.g., authoritarianism, hierarchy, control) at the expense of non-traditional elements (e.g., collaboration, coordination, problem solving) (see Willis, Mastrofski, & Weisburd, 2007). Moreover, there is some concern with regard to the pressures agencies face in terms of crime reporting (i.e., under reporting) and whether first-line supervisors and rank-and-file officers really buy-in or alter their behavior in any significant way (see Dabney, 2010; Eterno & Silverman, 2010).

Project Safe Neighborhoods (PSN)/Focused Deterrence

Since 2001, the U.S. Department of Justice has funded (now over $2 billion) an initiative called Project Safe Neighborhoods (PSN), which targets violent gang and gun crime. Prior to PSN, the Strategic Approaches to Community Safety Initiative (SACSI) was also funded by the U.S. Department of Justice (in 1998) in 10 participating cities. The SACSI model borrowed heavily on the problem-solving model and sought to draw on the successful practices from Operation Ceasefire in Boston (MA) and Project Exile in Richmond (VA). Presently operating in all 94 federal judicial districts, PSN revolves around a focused deterrence model associated with a pulling levers approach, whereby high-risk offenders (i.e., hot persons) and places (i.e., hot spots) are specifically targeted. As stated by Bonner, Worden, and McLean (2008: p. 1) "Focused deterrence—also known as 'lever pulling'—is a matter of enhancing the threat of criminal sanctions for the highest-risk offenders and deliberately communicating that threat in order to maximize its impact on offenders' behavior." Considered more broadly, most approaches using this model incorporate various elements of police-community partnerships, interagency working groups, research partnerships, deterrence messages, and the delivery of social services. As described by Braga and Weisburd (2007, p. 6):

> The pulling levers approach, in its simplest form, consists of selecting a particular crime problem, such as youth homicide; convening an interagency working group of law enforcement practitioners; conducting research to identify key offenders, groups, and behavior patterns; framing a response to offenders and groups of offenders that

uses a varied menu of sanctions ("pulling levers") to stop them from continuing their violent behavior; focusing social services and community resources on targeted offenders and groups to match law enforcement prevention efforts; and directly and repeatedly communicating with offenders to make them understand why they are receiving this special attention.

Various aspects of this policing strategy draw rather heavily on Goldstein's (1979, 1990) problem-solving process as a base. Moreover, multi-agency teams (or working groups) generally consist not only of federal, state, and local law enforcement practitioners (police and prosecution), but also other governmental agencies such as probation and parole. In addition, research partners (mainly university professors) are included as part of the working teams, assisting with training and data analyses (i.e., helping to identify high risk repeat offenders and places).

The deterrence message varies depending on the PSN federal district or city, as part of the appeal of this approach is adaptability to local conditions and preference. One popular approach is the use of offender notification meetings (often as part of his/her probation or parole status), where officials communicate to high-risk offenders that they are being explicitly targeted and that their criminal behavior will no longer be tolerated. Another approach is the use of a high-profile public education campaign involving multiple forms of media (e.g., radio, television, billboards, bus posters, etc.) to get the message out. In either form, officials essentially tell offenders that they can either stop offending or bear the brunt of the entire system (the collective resources of the working group), which may range from probation revocation for violating conditions to federal prosecution on gun charges and the likelihood of serious time incarcerated. While such tough talk (and subsequent action) is the "stick" part of pulling levers, offenders seeking to take such a message to heart are offered the proverbial "carrot" consisting of social services and community resources to help assist their path toward law abiding behavior.

According to McGarrell (2013), the most readily used PSN tactics include the establishment of criminal justice partnerships (100% of the 94 task forces) and federal prosecution of firearms (98%), while directed patrols of hot spots (58%) and offender notification meetings (45%) are used to a somewhat lesser degree. Overall, the pulling levers or focused-deterrence style of policing has been implemented and evaluated in a wide range of cities across the U.S., including Baltimore (MD), Boston (MA), Chicago, (IL), High Point (NC), Indianapolis (IN), Lowell (MA) and Minneapolis (MN). To date, studies in these cities have shown significant promise from a crime control perspective (see Braga & Weisburd, 2007 and McGarrell, 2013).

Intelligence-Led Policing (ILP)

Although it roots date back to the 1980s in England, Intelligence-Led Policing (ILP) did not begin to garner much attention in the U.S. until post 9/11. Some have gone so far (perhaps much too far) as to call ILP a new era in policing (Treverton et al., 2011). The underlying feature of this form of policing is obviously greater intelligence capability, but precisely what this means remains to some degree vague beyond the belief that information alone does not merit intelligence. Rather, one needs to combine information with analysis to create intelligence. Infrastructure changes at the federal level have sought to do this post 9/11, with state and local levels having a role. Twenty-five states currently operate fusion centers, which serve as a "clearinghouse for all potentially relevant, domestically generated homeland security data and information, leading to proper interpretation, assessment, and preventive actions" (Peterson, 2005: p 8). However, others see ILP as more than a terrorism-oriented policing strategy. Thus, alternatively referred to as both a management philosophy and business model, Ratcliffe (2003, p. 3) defines ILP as "the application of criminal intelligence analysis as an objective decision-making tool in order to facilitate crime reduction and prevention through effective policing strategies and external partnership projects drawn from an evidential base."

ILP seeks to incorporate many similar features as other evidence-based practices, and emphasizes the importance of data collection and analysis, developing and fostering collaborative relationships, and information sharing. At times there is also reference to ILP being part of, or leading to, what some call "predictive policing" based on the use of analytic and statistical technologies to enhance crime forecasts. It appears that ILP seeks to: hone in or focus more directly on using network type data collection and analysis, value the law enforcement function of the police (i.e., a narrow role) via the use of arrest, and be more person- or offender-focused than area or location based. Beyond this, however, the literature offers but a fairly abstract description as to the specifics of ILP and how it leads to a coherent policing strategy. Moreover, the extent to which ILP is effective is yet to be determined. Nonetheless, in 2009 the U.S. Department of Justice funded seven demonstration and evaluation projects in Boston (MA), Chicago (IL), Los Angeles (CA), State Police in Maryland, New York (NY), Shreveport (LA), and Washington Metropolitan (DC) (see Office of Justice Programs). Results from these projects are not yet available.

Strategic Management Analysis and Research Technology (SMART) Policing

The newest iteration of an evidence-based approach, SMART policing, began in 2009 with federal funding from the U.S. Department of Justice, Office of Justice Programs (OJP), and the Bureau of Justice Assistance (BJA). Presently, there are 33 police agencies nationally engaged in this form of policing (SMART Policing Initiative). Some of the agencies are large in size (Los Angeles, Philadelphia, Boston) while others smaller (Indio, California; Pharr, Texas; Shawneee, Kansas). At its broadest level, there are at least three primary components of SMART policing: strategic management (e.g., the measurement of goals and objectives, planning, information sharing), analysis and research (e.g., collecting and analyzing data, working with a research partner, outreach), and technology (e.g., crime mapping, link analyses). More directly, the overarching aim of SMART is to identify strategies and tactics that are both effective (e.g., reduce crime) and efficient (i.e., reduce crime while also being economical). Similar to PSN, a key component of the SMART initiative is for police agencies to link up with a local research partner, usually located at a nearby university. The SMART "team" then hones in on a crime category for which to focus, and identifies a primary technique of focusing on repeat offenders and/or problem places. For example, Baltimore, Boston, and Los Angeles identify gun crime as their primary problem. However, while Baltimore and Boston take an offender-based approach, Los Angeles takes a place-based approach. The research team then works to narrow the problem and identify specific strategies much like problem-oriented policing. Similar to ILP, the extent to which SMART policing is effective is yet to be determined, as objective peer-review studies of this initiative are ongoing.

Police Culture in the 21st Century

The current police culture state of affairs suggests that, once again, we are revisiting history. Much like the police operations in the community policing era resembled many of the characteristics of policing found in the political era, policing in the 21st century closely resembles aims of the professional era. That is, the current era's policing philosophy is going "back to the basics" in prioritizing efficient, bottom-line, approaches to fighting crime. So much so that police supervisors, especially at the upper echelons, are being personally held accountable for crime control efforts in their sectors, zones, districts, precincts, and bureaus. That being said, in theory, the current approach is different in that there is not a driving need to separate the police and the public from corrupt relationships, like that of the professional era. Although, larger public safety threats that require police to be alert and monitor/surveil citizens, disorderly (or "out of place") conditions, and mass gatherings, during the current era, might lead to similar unintended consequences as that noted during the reform era. At the same time, remnants of community policing are still hanging around, in varying degrees, across American police agencies.

From a police culture standpoint, the environments, coping mechanisms, and outcomes of the occupational perspective (Paoline, 2003) that were theoretically being undone during the prior community era are once again salient in 2013. At the same time though, the past era is close enough in proximity, and even if departments are no longer prioritizing such initiatives, officers are still around that were exposed to community policing philosophies and are now senior patrol members, FTOs, and supervisors, responsible for socializing others. This suggests that the door is currently wide open for officers to culturally adapt to the strains of the job in a variety of ways; some that might be like past methods or new approaches altogether. How officers interpret their internal and external work environments, and the ways in which they respond to such conditions, either collectively or individually, is unknown.

Concluding Thought

Despite some future questions yet to be resolved, there is no question that the policing field, as illustrated above, has evolved and become more evidence based. Nonetheless, to date, the success stories still fall in the minority. While many agencies (small, medium, and large) have witnessed some extraordinary changes, make no mistake that the primary everyday policing strategy remains very much the same as it has for well over the past 50-plus years. Random preventative patrol is still, by far, the predominant policing strategy despite the lack of scientific evidence regarding its ineffectiveness. Every day, in countless police departments across the country, police officers get into marked vehicles and randomly patrol their service beats responding to calls for service. One can talk all day about hot spots, or Compstat, or SMART policing, but the vast majority of police officer behavior has not been substantially altered by such programs, even if scholars and police leaders like to pay homage to them. At the same time, as demonstrated in this chapter, the philosophical changes in police operations across time have had implications for the formation and degree of collectiveness of police culture(s).

References

Bonner, H. S., Worden, R. E., & McLean, S. J. (2008). *Focused deterrence initiatives: A synopsis.* Albany, NY: Finn Institute.

Braga, A. A., & Bond, B. J. (2008). Policing crime and disorder hot spots: A randomized controlled trial. *Criminology, 46,* 577–607.

Braga, A. A., & Weisburd, D. L. (2007). *Police innovation and crime prevention: Lessons learned from police research over the past 20 years.* Paper presented at the National Institute of Justice (NIJ) Policing research workshop: Planning for the future, Washington, DC, November 28–29, 2006.

Braga, A, Papachristos, A. A., & Hureau, D. (2012). *Hot spots policing effects on crime.* Campbell systematic review 2012:8 DOI: 10.40.4091/csr.2012.8.

Bureau of Justice Assistance. (2013). Retrieved from https://www.bja.gov/eval uation/program-law-enforcement/place-based1.htm on April 30, 2013.

Chappell, A. T., Monk-Turner, E., & Payne, B. K. (2011). Broken windows or window breakers: The influence of physical and social disorder on quality of life. *Justice Quarterly, 28,* 522–540.

Dabney, D. (2010). Observations regarding key operational realities in a compstat model of policing. *Justice Quarterly, 27,* 28–51.

Eck, J. E., & Spelman, W. (1987). *Problem solving: Problem-oriented policing in Newport News.* Washington, DC: Police Executive Research Forum.

Eck, J. E., Chainey, S., Cameron, J. G., Leitner, M., & Wilson, R. E. (2005). *Mapping crime: Understanding hot spots.* Washington, DC: U.S. Department of Justice, Office of Justice Programs, National Institute of Justice.

Escobedo v. Illinois, 378 U.S. 478 (1964).

Eskridge, C. (1989). College and the police: A review of the issues. In D.J. Kenney (Ed.), *Police and policing: Contemporary issues* (pp. 17–25). New York, NY: Praeger.

Eterno, J. A., & Silverman, E. B. (2010). The NYPD's compstat: Compare statistics or compose statistics? *International Journal of Police Science & Management, 12,* 426–449.

Fosdick, R. B. (1920). *American police systems.* New York, NY: The Century Company.

Goldstein, H. (1979). Improving policing: A problem-oriented approach. *Crime and Delinquency, 24,* 236–58.

Goldstein, H. (1990). *Problem-oriented policing.* New York, NY: McGraw Hill.

Gould, L. L. (2001). *America in the progressive era, 1890-1914.* Harlow, UK: Pearson Publishing.

Greene, J. R. (2004). Community policing and organization change. In W. Skogan (Ed.), *Community policing: Can it work?* (pp. 30–53). Belmont, CA: Wadsworth Publishing.

Greenwood, P. W., & Petersilia, J. (1975). *The criminal investigation process.* Vol. 1, *Summary and policy implications.* Santa Monica, CA: Rand.

Haller, M. (1976). Historical roots of police behavior: Chicago, 1890–1925. *Law and Society Review, 10,* 303–24.

Kelling, G. L., Pate, T., Dieckman, D., & Brown, C. E. (1974). *The Kansas City preventive patrol experiment: A summary report.* Washington, DC: The Police Foundation.

Lane, R. (1967). *Policing the city: Boston, 1822-1885.* Cambridge, MA: Harvard University Press.

London Metropolitan Police. (2013). Retrieved from http://content.met.police.uk on April 18, 2013.

Mapp v. Ohio, 367 U.S. 643 (1961).

Martin, S. E. (1997). Women officers on the move: An update on women in policing. In R. G. Dunham & G. P. Alpert (Eds.) *Critical issues in policing* (3rd Edition). Prospect Heights, IL: Waveland Press Incorporated.

Mastrofski, S. D., Worden, R. E., & Snipes, J. B. (1995). Law enforcement in a time of community policing. *Criminology, 33,* 539–563.

McGarrell, E. F. (2013). Offender-oriented strategies: The focused deterrence 'pulling levers' strategy. In G. Bruinsma & D. Weisburd (Eds.). *Encyclopedia of criminology and criminal justice.* New York, NY: Springer-Verlag Publishing.

Miller, W. (1977). *Cops and bobbies: Police authority in New York and London, 1830–1870.* Chicago, IL: University of Chicago Press.

Miranda v. Arizona, 384 U.S. 436 (1966).

Monkkonen, E. H. (1992). History of urban police. In M. Tonry & N. Morris (Eds.), *Crime and Justice, Volume 15* (pp. 547–580). Chicago, IL: University of Chicago Press.

Office of Justice Programs. Retrieved from http://www.ojp.gov/funding/pdfs/FY2009221.pdf on May 1, 2013.

Paoline, E. A., III. (2003). Taking stock: Toward a richer understanding of police culture. *Journal of Criminal Justice, 31,* 199–214.

Paoline, E. A., III, Myers, S. M., & Worden, R. E. (2000). Police culture, individualism, and community policing: Evidence from two police departments. *Justice Quarterly, 17,* 575–605.

Paoline, E. A., III, & Terrill, W. (2007). Police education, experience, and the use of force. *Criminal Justice and Behavior, 34,* 179–196.

Peterson, M. (2005). *Intelligence-led policing: The new intelligence architecture.* Washington, DC: U.S. Department of Justice, Office of Justice Programs, Bureau of Justice Assistance.

Ratcliffe, J. H. (2003). *Intelligence-led policing.* Canberra, Australia: Australian Institute of Criminology.

Reaves, B. (2010). *Law enforcement management and administrative statistics: Local police departments, 2007.* Washington, DC: U.S. Department of Justice, Office of Justice Programs, Bureau of Justice Statistics.

Roth, J. A., Roehl, J., & Johnson, C. C. (2004). Trends in community policing. In W. Skogan (Ed.), *Community policing: Can it work?* (pp. 3–29). Belmont, CA: Wadsworth publishing.

Sherman, L. W. (1998). *Evidence-based policing.* Washington, DC: Police Foundation.

Sherman, L. W. (2013). Targeting, testing and tracking police services: The rise of evidence-based policing, 1975–2025. In M. Tonry (Ed.), *Crime and Justice, Volume 42* (pp. 1–61). Chicago, IL: University of Chicago Press.

Sherman, L. W., Gartin, P. R., & Buerger, M. E. (1989). Hot spots of predatory crime: Routine activities and the criminology of place. *Criminology, 7,* 27–55.

Skogan, W. G., & Steiner, L. (2004). *Community policing in Chicago, year 10: An evaluation of Chicago's alternative policing strategy.* Illinois Criminal Justice Information Authority.

Skolnick, J. H. (1969). *The politics of protest.* New York, NY: Simon and Schuster.

SMART Policing Initiative. Retrieved from http://www.smartpolicinginitiative.com on May 2, 2013.

Spelman, W. & Brown, D. K. (1984). *Calling the police: Citizen reporting of serious crime.* Washington, DC: U.S. Government Printing Office.

Treverton, G. F., Wollman, M. Wilke, E. & Lai, D. (2011). *Moving toward the future of policing.* Santa Monica, CA: RAND Corporation.

U.S. Census Bureau. Retrieved from census.gov on April 14, 2013.

Walker, S. (1977). *A critical history of police reform: The emergence of professionalism.* Lexington, MA: Lexington Books.

Walker, S. (1980). *Popular justice: A history of American criminal justice.* New York, NY: Oxford University Press.

Weisburd, D. Mastrofski, S. D., McNally, A. M., Greenspan, R. & Willis, J. J. (2003). Reforming to preserve: Compstat and strategic problem solving in American policing. *Criminology & Public Policy, 2,* 421–456.

Weisburd, D., Telep, C. W., Hinkle, J. C., & Eck, J. E. (2010). Is problem-oriented policing effective in reducing crime and disorder? *Criminology and Public Policy, 9,* 139–172.

Westley, W. A. (1970). *Violence and the police: A sociological study of law, custom, and morality*. Cambridge, MA: MIT Press.

White, S. O. (1972). A perspective on police professionalization. *Law & Society Review, 7*, 61–85.

Willis, J. J., Mastrofski, S. D., & Weisburd, D. (2007). Making sense of compstat: A theory based analysis of organizational change in three police departments. *Law & Society Review, 41*, 147–188.

Wilson, J. Q. (1968). *Varieties of police behavior: The management of law and order in eight communities*. Cambridge, MA: Harvard University Press.

Wilson, J. Q., & Kelling, G. (1982). Broken windows: The police and neighborhood safety. *The Atlantic Monthly*, 29–38.

Wilson, O. W. (1950). *Police administration*. New York, NY: McGraw-Hill.

Chapter 3

The External and Internal Environments of Seven Departments

The seven police departments that serve as the arenas to examine police culture were part of a larger *National Institute of Justice*-funded study geared toward assessing the impact of different use of force policies on a number of theoretically relevant outcomes. These outcomes included: officer policy perceptions, frequency (and levels) of force usage, citizen complaints, citizen injuries, officer injuries, and civil lawsuits. In choosing these sites, our primary aim was to ensure that each department varied in the way that they were instructing their officers in utilizing coercion over citizens. Another aim was to consider organizational variation based on factors such as size and structure.

As part of our multimethod project, the research team conducted a series of open-ended interviews, using a snowball method, with several personnel of varying ranks and assignments (e.g., patrol officers, middle managers, top-level executives, trainers, special tactics personnel, public information officers, internal affairs, etc.) in an effort to detail the overall operation of each of these organizations (e.g., internal structure, policies and procedures, supervisory review, external community, etc.). The site visits occurred over a two-year period, from 2006–2008, with at least one month of total time at each location. In addition to the time spent physically on site, we were in constant contact with agency personnel throughout the study period via phone, email, and postal mail. While our structured survey of patrol officers (see Chapter 4 for detail on this process) serves as a primary source of data for examining police culture, the unstructured (and structured) meetings and interviews illuminated a number of important aspects regarding how these organizations operated and the communities they served. We draw on this information to provide a thumbnail sketch of these seven agencies.

Similar to prior conceptualizations of police culture (as outlined in Chapter 1), we utilized a variety of research methodologies to learn about the environments of the departments. As such, the information used for descriptions of the internal organizational environments and the external community was gathered from several oral and written sources (e.g., discussions, interviews, observations, formal written policies, agency memorandums, city websites, annual reports, etc.). Some of the written description that follows is taken directly from prior and/or existing documents, while other material is taken and pieced together from a variety of data sources. As a result, we do not always apply traditional quotations around every direct source and/or quote. Admittedly, some of the material is that of the city, agency, website, or other source. Our primary task was to first understand the vast structural characteristics and processes occurring in each of the different cultural arenas before being able to document such dynamics, with the intent to provide a proper context to what we analyze. As such, our goal was not to create and write a detailed historical and complete contemporary description that focused on source specificity, but instead to offer a background setting across the seven agencies. Within this context, we apologize to any person or entity whose material may be presented here without any or full attribution.

A second caveat involves the use of multiple police departments. While it is common to hear in an introductory research methods class, or read in a discussion section of a journal article, *replication across a number of organizations would enhance the findings reported here from a single organization*, sometimes the practical realities of multi-site investigations are cumbersome and/or problematic. That is, what you do for one, you have to do for all. In keeping to this mantra, we provide equal descriptions of some primary dimensions of context for the external and internal environments across sites. On the one hand this provides symmetry, while on the other you lose some individual-level detail because of the inability to uniformly capture something across all agencies. Because of our multi-site approach, we err on the side of consistency across agencies in our descriptions. In doing so, we describe community context from which these police agencies were operating, and then detail primary factors of organizational size and structure.

The External Environments

In the course of our site visits, and off-site correspondence with our agency contacts, we gleaned a good deal of information about the cities. With respect to police culture, this represents the external occupational environment, and one of the two main arenas (along with the organizational) where outlooks are shaped. Before detailing how each of the departments was organized (by size and structure), we begin with a comparison of the communities in which policing operated in these seven sites. In accomplishing this aim, we concentrate on aggregate population characteristics, crime levels, workloads, use of force frequencies, and relative danger. Table 3.1 (on the following page) lists each of our cities and how they compared across these factors.

In terms of overall policing populations, our seven sites provide substantial variation, ranging from 182,337 in Knoxville to 733,291 in Charlotte-Mecklenburg. Across the cities we also have categories of size, which correspond to the number of sworn personnel (see agency descriptions below) that allow for groupings of larger (Columbus and Charlotte-Mecklenburg), medium (Portland, Albuquerque, and Colorado Springs), and smaller (Fort Wayne and Knoxville).

Across a variety of socioeconomic distress (McCluskey, Mastrofski, & Parks, 1999) or concentrated disadvantage indicators (Sampson, Raudenbush, & Earls, 1997), we see that in some instances we have tight clustering among sites, while for other measures we see more disparity. For example, percent unemployed (ranging from 3.1 in Colorado Springs to 4.5 in Portland) and percentage of female-headed households (ranging from 6.3 in Portland to 9.8 in Fort Wayne) are more closely situated than the percentage of population below the poverty level (ranging from 6.1 in Colorado Springs to 14.4 in Knoxville) and percentage of population that is non-White (ranging from 19.3 in Colorado Springs to 36.0 in Charlotte-Mecklenburg).

In terms of relative crime levels (i.e., Part I crimes per 1,000 population) we see greater diversity, ranging from 49.5 in Colorado Springs to 81.8 in Knoxville. Interestingly, in most agencies, except Knoxville our smallest in population and sworn personnel, crime levels positively correspond to size (i.e., the greater the population and sworn personnel, the greater the crime).

With respect to officer workload, we find variation in calls for service. Unlike the preceding figures that were based on one year (of our two on site), calls for service are combined for both years. Again, levels of calls for service correspond to size, as our most populated sites (Columbus and Charlotte-Mecklenburg) have two to three times the number of calls than our smallest cities (Fort Wayne and Knoxville).

Table 3.1 · The External Environments of Study Sites

	Columbus	Charlotte-Mecklenburg	Portland	Albuquerque	Colorado Springs	Fort Wayne	Knoxville
Population	733,203	733,291	538,133	513,124	374,112	248,423	182,337
Percent Non-White	32.0	36.0	22.1	28.4	19.3	24.5	20.3
Percent Female Headed	9.3	7.6	6.3	8.0	7.1	9.8	8.0
Percent Below Poverty	10.8	6.6	8.5	10.0	6.1	9.6	14.4
Percent Unemployed	3.5	3.7	4.5	3.8	3.1	4.3	3.9
Part I Crimes/ 1,000 Population	78.8	79.8	65.5	66.9	49.5	43.6	81.8
Calls for Service	1,528,280	810,423	446,869	652,366	538,280	354,175	446,161
Use of Force/ 1,000 Calls	3.8	4.6	9.8	2.2	1.4	5.6	2.1
Percentage of Force Encs. Officer Injured	8.1	13.4	9.0	*	12.7	12.2	14.8

*Albuquerque did not collect official data on officer injuries.

As a measure of aggregate dangerousness across the sites, we document officially reported use of force utilized by officers per 1,000 calls for service and the percentage of force encounters in which officers documented that they were injured. Like calls for service calculation, these measures utilize data from our two years combined on site. Use of force per 1,000 calls for service varied from 1.4 in Colorado Springs to 9.8 in Portland. Interestingly, our largest sites did not account for the most use of force per 1,000 calls for service. In terms of officers receiving physical injuries during their use of force encounters with suspects, even though the percentages are low with a tightly grouped range, our fewest injuries were reported in one of our largest sites (8.1 in Columbus) and the most injuries were found in our smallest site (14.8 in Knoxville).

Overall, the external environments are rich arenas for exploring the ways in which officers respond to the strains of the occupation, providing enough variation to be different from one another, but not so diverse that comparisons cannot be made across sites. Next, we explore the internal facets of the organizational environments for which patrol officers worked, with a concentration on their size (i.e., small, medium, and large in terms of sworn personnel) and structure (i.e., overall administration, patrol, shifts, promotions, unions, specialized units, and supervisory oversight for police action).

Columbus (Ohio) Police Department

The Columbus Police Department (CPD), with 1,819 sworn personnel, represents the largest of the seven agencies. Of the 1,819 sworn personnel, 910 were assigned to street level patrol assignments, which is the highest percentage (50%) of all sites. CPD also had the most police officers per 1,000 residents (2.48).

Administrative Structure

CPD's overall organizational structure is not overly complicated or busy for a large police department. The department consists of five subdivisions that operate under the chief of police, each of which is headed by a deputy chief. The Administrative Subdivision includes four bureaus: Business & Personnel, Training, Professional Standards, and Internal Affairs. The Investigative Subdivision includes four bureaus: Crimes Against Persons, Narcotics, Property Crimes, and Special Victims. The Patrol East Subdivision includes four units: Patrol Zones 1, 2, 5, and Homeland Security. The Patrol West Subdivision includes three units: Patrol Zones 3 and 4, and Traffic Bureau. The Support Services Subdivision includes four bureaus: Communications, Special Services, Strategic Response, and Technical Services. Each bureau, or zone of patrol, that operates within each subdivision is headed by a commander.

Patrol Geographic and Shift Structure

The highest level of patrol aggregation in Columbus is the zone. CPD has five patrol zones, which span the aforementioned East and West subdivisions. The East Subdivision includes zones 1, 2, and 5, while the West Subdivision covers zones 3 and 4. Across the five patrol zones there are 19 precincts that are housed in 13 separate police stations. As such, CPD's spatial differentiation (i.e., the geographic distribution of police across the city) (Langworthy, 1986; Maguire, 2003) is among the highest of all agencies. In terms of supervision, CPD assigns one sergeant per precinct per shift, whose span of control covers 8-12 officers. Roll calls before the start of each shift are conducted by precinct sergeants. Each patrol shift also has a designated watch lieutenant.

CPD operates on three primary 8-hour shifts/watches (first, second, and third), with early and late reporting times across precincts. Early-reporting precinct shifts start at 0600, 1400, and 2200 (precincts 18, 7, 9, 11, 8, 10, 1, 17, 4, and 5), while late-reporting precinct shifts start at 0700, 1500, and 2300 (precincts 2, 14, 13, 12, 19, 15, 16, 3, and 6). The department also has two additional midwatch shifts — day (0900–1900) and evening (1830–0430), which do not meet at all precincts, but instead meet at one designated precinct per zone.

Promotional Structure

There are five rank designations above the patrol level (i.e., sergeant, lieutenant, commander, deputy chief, and chief). For a large police agency, this measure of vertical differentiation (Langworthy, 1986; Maguire, 2003) is somewhat small. CPD's promotional process is civil service, and the safety director generally makes appointments off the promotion list. CPD's promotion list is good for two years. From the position of commander up, promotions are more selective. Patrol officers in CPD must be on duty for three years before they can take the test to become a sergeant. Each subsequent post requires a year at the position before an officer can take a test for the next promotion. CPD has educational requirements (i.e., baccalaureate degree) in place for promotion starting at the commander rank. CPD's sergeant and lieutenant promotional exams have four parts: open-book multiple choice exam, a closed-book multiple choice exam, a work sample component, and an oral board component. For commander and deputy chief promotions, there are two parts: a work sample component and an oral board component. All non-written portions of the process are videotaped and evaluated by a second panel of raters.

Specialized Units

Functional differentiation refers to "the degree to which tasks are broken down into functionally distinct units" (Maguire, 2003, p. 15). The department has a number of specialized units (i.e., CPD is functionally differentiated) that operate primarily out of the Special Services Bureau of the Support Services Subdivision. These units include: Marine-Park Unit, Underwater Search and Recovery Unit, Helicopter Unit, SWAT Unit, and K-9 Unit. The department also has a Strategic Response Bureau, which has community liaison officers (one assigned to each precinct). "Walkie" Units (i.e., foot patrol) for downtown and campus areas also exist (out of Patrol). Out of the Traffic Bureau of the Patrol West Subdivision, there is a Mounted Unit and Motorcycle Unit, while out of the Homeland Security Section of the Patrol East Subdivision there is the Emergency Management Unit and Terrorism Early Warning Unit.

Unions/Collective Bargaining

Sworn personnel up though the commander rank are unionized under the Fraternal Order of Police (FOP). CPD's union is regarded as very strong, according to several organizational members. At one point, the Department of Justice wanted to impose a consent decree, but the union refused. As part of this process, officers collectively agreed to contribute parts of their individual pay to assist in legal fees.

Supervisory Oversight for Use of Force Documentation and Complaints

CPD's use of force policy, which they label The Action-Response to Resistance/ Aggression (to avoid negative connotations), mandates that an official report be filled out every time an officer uses force. For the lowest levels of force (levels 0-1 — which include commands, searching, handcuffing, sparking the Taser®, soft hand techniques), the officer completes a use of force form and forwards it to his/her immediate supervisor. If the use force level is Level

3 (use of a Taser®), 4 (hard hand strikes), 5 (batons/flashlights), 6 (K-9), and 7 (bean bags, knee knockers, sting balls—less lethal control), or if someone is injured (at any level of force), the supervisor conducts an investigation, reviews the officer's use of force report, and recommends discipline (if any). The use of force report, filed by the officer, is reviewed by the chain of command (i.e., all ranks above the officer) and the deputy chief makes the final determination regarding the appropriateness of the officer's actions. When officers use deadly force (Level 8), all of the investigating and report writing takes place by their immediate supervisor.

CPD's Internal Affairs (IA) keeps all records for use of force (above levels 0 and 1, which are stored and used for training purposes in the academy), complaints, and injuries to prisoners. When officers' use of force is investigated by the front-line supervisor, the only action taken by IA is to receive and file it. If a citizen complaint is attached to the use of force incident, then IA will open an investigation.

Complaints against CPD officers can come from internal (i.e., other officers and supervisors) and external (i.e., citizens) sources. Following investigations by IA (for citizen complaints and very serious internal complaints) or chain of command (for most internal complaints), a complaint may be classified as: cancelled for cause (i.e., it is obvious the alleged misconduct could not possibly occurred or subject of complaint is not a departmental employee), unable to resolve (i.e., not enough information to complete the investigation), withdrawn, policy/procedure (i.e., the alleged conduct did occur, but the officer was following approved policy or procedure or was following a direct order from a supervisor), unfounded, not sustained, and sustained.

IA handles all complaints from citizens, and internal complaints when a chain of command investigation will not suffice. Once a valid citizen complaint has been made and logged, it is assigned to an IA investigator. The investigator sends a notice to the complainant and a summary of the complaint is written and sent to investigator's chain of command for review. The involved officer is notified via email and the chain of command is copied. The officer is not notified if it is an ongoing conduct investigation. The IA investigator investigates and recommends a finding. An investigation is sometimes reviewed by the bureau commander if it is a sustained finding, a noteworthy case, or a use of force complaint. The chain of command handles discipline after IA completes the investigation, and the deputy chief is the final authority. The chief of police examines the report if the recommendation is for a formal charge.

Internal complaints, which have to be made in writing, are handled by a chain of command investigation, or IA if it is deemed that the chain of command investigation will not suffice. Internal complaints have to be made within 60 days of the alleged incident. The process for internal complaints is much less detailed, suggesting that the chain of command has tremendous discretion and latitude in handling these incidents.

Discipline against CPD officers can come in one of the following forms: positive corrective action, documented constructive counseling, written reprimand, and departmental charges (which include leave forfeiture, suspension, demotion, termination). The majority of CPD's disciplinary actions taken are "document of constructive counseling" or "formal reprimand" (sergeants and higher have the power to do this). The highest level of discipline involves departmental charges against the officer (i.e., leave, suspension, demotion, or termination), but can only be done by the chief (with recommendations from the chain of command). Once a disposition is determined, IA closes the complaint and sends a notice to the complainant and the officer. An appeal of findings can be made by the officer through the deputy chief. If the disposition is appealed by the officer, an arbitrator gets involved in the process.

CPD officers have the power to appeal documented constructive counseling or written reprimands per the grievance process in the current collective bargaining contract. A more formalized process (union and legal representation) can be done in front of the chief for departmental charges. Decisions from the meeting with the chief can be appealed to the director of public safety.

In terms of tracking potentially problematic officer behavior (i.e., Early Warning or Early Intervention systems) (Walker, 2003), CPD utilizes the Employee Action Review System (EARS) program. This system is based primarily on officers' use of force and citizen complaints. New recruits are trained about EARS at the police academy, as are new supervisors. CPD officers are subject to EARS based on a percentage of all uses of force (if an officer is in the 95th percentile, he or she is subject to review). CPD's EARS committee looks at all the involved reports for an officer and makes a decision via a vote. If there is a problem, then a plan of action for the officer is implemented. The EARS committee response is officially documented in the officer's master personnel file. An annual review is conducted by EARS each year by officers' immediate supervisors, which details: personnel actions (i.e., awards, compliments, assignment changes, absence without leave), IA reviewable activities (i.e., citizen complaints, Equal Employment Opportunity complaints, use of firearms, action-response to resistance/aggression, injury to prisoner, strip searches, criminal investigations, internal investigations, and forced entry), legal advisor office activities (i.e., civil claims against the agency and civil claims against the officer), and employee chain of command information (i.e., type of assignment and contacts and whether they are positive or negative).

Charlotte-Mecklenburg (North Carolina) Police Department

The Charlotte-Mecklenburg Police Department (CMPD) represents our second largest police department with 1,638 sworn personnel. CMPD has 685 officers assigned to street-level patrol, representing 42 percent of all sworn employees. Of our seven departments, CMPD has the second most (to CPD) officers assigned per 1,000 residents (2.23).

Administrative Structure

Compared to our other large police agency (CPD), CMPD is much more functionally differentiated (Langworthy, 1986; Maguire, 2003), with a number of organizational layers of bureaus and units. At the top of CMPD's organizational hierarchy is the Chief's Office, which houses three units: Internal Affairs, Public Affairs, and the Police Attorney(s). At the first layer beneath the Chief's Office are four groups: Field Services Group, Investigative Services Group, Support Services Group, and Administrative Services Group. Each of these groups is headed by a deputy chief. The Field Services Group includes: the seven Patrol Service Areas (each headed by a major), the Field Services Support Unit (headed by a sergeant), the School Resource Officer Unit (headed by a sergeant), and departmental chaplains. The Investigative Services Group includes: the Special Investigations Bureau and the Criminal Investigations Bureau, both of which are headed by a major. The Support Services Group includes: the Special Operations Bureau (headed by a major), the Community Services Bureau (headed by a major), and the Crime Lab Division. The Administrative Services Group includes: the Human Resources Division, Training (headed by a captain) the Recruiting Division, the Fiscal Affairs Division, the Professional Standards Unit (headed by a sergeant), and the Administrative Services Bureau (headed by a major).

Patrol Geographic and Shift Structure

Patrol allocation spans seven primary service areas that house 13 separate divisional police stations. As such, CMPD (like CPD) is characterized by a high degree of functional differentiation. The seven service areas, each headed by a captain, include: Central Service Area (Central Division), West Service Area (Metro Division and Freedom Division), Southeast Service Area (Hickory Grove Division and Independence Division), North Service Area (North Division and University City Division), East Service Area (Eastway Division and North Tryon Division), South Service Area (Providence Division and South Division), and Southwest Service Area (Steele Creek Division and Westover Division). Within each of the 13 divisions are three primary response areas (i.e., beats). CMPD officers are assigned permanently to a response area within their division. Each CMPD division also has one investigative technician and three community coordinators assigned to them. Once a recruit finishes the police academy, s/he is assigned to a division following a draft among division captains. Division need is assessed by a workload formula that considers area in square miles, available officers, citizens, and calls for service.

Patrol shifts vary across each of the 13 divisions, with alternating start times and numbers per division (i.e., anywhere from five to six). There are three primary patrol shifts (e.g., 0600–1410, 1400–2210, 2200–0615) and overlapping shifts for morning and/or evening in one division (i.e., University City). CMPD's 5th shift has a mid-morning start time (between 0900–1045) and is usually reserved for officers assigned to radar, bike, and school resource units. Officers work eight-hour shifts with two days off per week, except for the 4th shift which is a 10-hour shift. Roll calls, which are headed by a sergeant who runs each shift, are conducted at each division at the start of each shift.

Promotional Structure

There are five promotions (post patrol) that occur—sergeant, captain, major, deputy chief, and chief, which for a large police department does not represent a large degree of vertical differentiation (Langworthy, 1986; Maguire, 2003). For promotions to the ranks of sergeant and captain, CMPD utilizes a method of combining scores from written and oral interviews to hierarchically order eligibility. Sergeant candidates are rank ordered and chosen according to one's placement on this list. Captain promotions are done via the "rule of five," which is a system by which any one of the top five candidates can be picked by the chief of police regardless of his/her individual ranking. The system for the rank of major can deviate from this plan and be made on an individual basis (i.e., per each application process). Promotional recommendations for sergeant, captain, and major are subject to approval from the civil service board. Deputy chief promotions are made at the discretion of the chief of police, as this is an appointed position.

Specialized Units

Like most large police organizations, CMPD has a number of specialized units, most of which operate within the Special Operations Bureau. These include: Highway Intervention and Traffic Safety (HITS), Motorcycle Unit, Street Crimes Division, Canine Unit, Aviation Unit and Civil Energy Unit, SWAT Team, Advanced Local Emergency Response Team (ALERT), Bomb Squad Unit, Cyber Crimes Unit, Crime Prevention Unit. CMPD also has specialized units within the Field Services Group, including: Bike Patrol and School Resource Officers (SRO). Finally, the Special Investigations Bureau (under Investigative Services Group) houses specialized units such as: Narcotics Unit, Violent Crimes Unit, Gang Intelligence Unit, Conspiracy Unit, Vice Technical Unit, and ABC Unit.

Unions/Collective Bargaining

CMPD is not unionized and is not permitted to collectively bargain per the city charter. As such, there is not a city contract for police employees. There are two fraternal organizations, the FOP and Police Benevolent Association (PBA), which will provide legal counseling for officers (if requested). The most common counseling is for police-involved shootings. Officers, who belong to one of these organizations, are provided legal counseling before they speak to Internal Affairs (IA), but union representatives are not allowed to be present during officer-IA meetings. CMPD officers are protected under civil service, in that any promotion, termination, or suspension must be approved by the civil service board. This five-member board is appointed by the mayor. Patrol officers through the rank of major are part of civil service, while the deputy chief and chief are not.

Supervisory Oversight for Use of Force Documentation and Complaints

CMPD mandates that officers fill out a use of force form for the following situations: force that causes any visible injury to (or complaint from) a suspect, hands on force, use of baton or flashlight (or other impact weapons) to strike a suspect, any blow to the head, OC spray, Taser®, any type of less lethal force when an arrest is made, canine bites, suspect loses consciousness, and discharging a firearm. Officers are required to contact their supervisor immediately after using force; this supervisor then conducts an investigation of the incident (Supervisor Investigative Report). The supervisor completes the report based on information provided by the officer(s) and citizen(s) at the scene (via an investigation).

Once the supervisor, usually a sergeant, conducts the use of force investigation, s/he makes a recommendation regarding whether or not the officer's actions were justified. Investigations are then sent up the chain of command (division captain to service area major, and the IA captain serves as a check over the process for consistency and oversight), where each person who reviews the incident deems it justified or unjustified force. The final disposition comes from the service area major. Electronic tracking is done for each use of force incident, which documents who reviewed the case, their comments, and for how long. There is a 45-day limit imposed on reviews of use of force incidents.

Complaints against officers can be both internal and external. Following an investigation, a complaint is classified as: sustained, not sustained, unfounded, or exonerated. Field supervisors generally investigate complaints against their subordinates, while IA investigates complaints related to use of force, pursuits, conduct unbecoming, corruption, abuse of position, and insubordination. IA oversees all investigations, even those that they are not directly involved in. Final dispositions and discipline are handled by the officer's chain of command. Direct supervisors are usually the first ones notified about a complaint against a subordinate, and they are also responsible for acknowledging the alleged complaint in writing. Like use of force reviews, all complaint cases against officers are required to be disposed of within 45 days.

Disciplinary reviews are conducted by the chain of command for all investigations done by IA. If it is deemed by IA that misconduct did occur, disposition is decided by a chain of command review board. The chief of police has the option to decide final disposition in any disciplinary manner. Officers have the option to request a chain of command hearing for any completed complaint investigation. For any chain of command review board, the accused officer can elect to have a peer serve on the board as a member (usually from the same job classification). Officers who have counsel are not permitted to have them present during the review.

Criminal investigations of misconduct are not done by IA, but instead by the criminal investigation unit. Officers can be polygraphed and are subject to searches of their police property. Officers are notified in writing of final dispositions, and they can respond in writing and it will be included in the electronic file as well as their personnel file. Disciplinary suspensions can be appealed to the civil service board as long as the officer has completed his/her probationary period. Appeals have to be made within 15 days of officer notification of suspension. The major of IA is responsible for responding to the civil service board. If the investigation results in the firing of an officer, s/he must be notified in writing why s/he was fired, the effective date of the dismissal, and notification to human resources to cover the status of fringe/retirement benefits. Probationary officers can be terminated by the chief, and while they cannot appeal to the civil service board they may file a grievance, per the city grievance procedures.

Complaints reviewed by the chain of command are usually disciplined by them, while IA investigations are investigatory only as the chain of command and chief handle discipline. The chief can override the chain of command reviewing body and discipline as s/he deems appropriate. Officers can appeal disciplinary sanctions to the civil service board when a suspension (or deferred suspension) is the punishment, although this must be done within 15 days of notice. Officers can also grieve any disciplinary action to the city via the city grievance policy. Officers are not permitted to grieve a suspension that is also being appealed to the civil service board. Disciplinary actions usually involve one or more of the following: counseling, active suspension, inactive suspension, termination, resignation, written reprimand.

CMPD has a clearly specified Early Intervention (EI) system, which is geared toward identifying at-risk behaviors and activities before formal discipline is needed. EI system records are a permanent part of personnel records, but information is purged from the electronic system for each employee five years after the alert. Qualifying EI system incidents include on-duty vehicle accidents (2 in 180 days), injuries (2 in 180 days), citizen and departmental complaints (3 in 180 days), use of force (3 in 90 days), vehicle pursuits (2 in 180 days), sick leave in conjunction with days off (2 in 90 days), sick leave in conjunction with vacation (2 in 90 days), sick leave frequency (2 in 90 days), or a combination of any of the above (5 in 180 days).

Once an officer meets the EI system threshold for one of the above actions, a supervisor does a review/evaluation. Supervisors can mandate one or more of the following after their review: defensive tactics instruction, communication skills development, supervisor counseling, one-on-one training or course instruction, or Employee Assistance Program (EAP). Much of this system is left up to the discretion of the officer's supervisor. Supervisors are also charged with evaluating the need for post-intervention assessments, which are reviewed by the chain of command. Officers can review their history at any time and are alerted once the system is triggered (i.e., a threshold is met). The EI system has a review panel made up of various departmental employees who evaluate the system and report to the chief. IA is the repository for all EI system records, and monthly EI system reports are generated.

Portland (Oregon) Police Bureau

The Portland Police Bureau (PPB), with 989 sworn officers, represents one of our three mid-sized police agencies. PPB allocates 382, of its 989 sworn employees, to street-level patrol positions, which is the lowest percentage (39) of all sites. PPB has 1.84 police per 1,000 residents, which ranks among the fewest of the seven agencies (i.e., tied for 5th).

Administrative Structure

PPB's organizational structure is functionally differentiated, with a number of specialized units (subdivided under several divisions) located within the three primary branches. At the top of the organization is the Chief's Office, which houses: Support Staff, Chief's Forum, and PPB Advisory Board; Adjutant Lieutenant (with mayor protection); Planning and Support; Criminal Intelligence; and Public Information. PPB's primary branches, located beneath the Chief's Office, are Services, Investigations, and Operations. The Services Branch consists of six divisions (Fiscal Services, Personnel, Records, Training, Management Services, and Information Technology), the Investigations Branch consists of seven divisions (Drugs & Vice, Family Services, Property/Evidence, Internal Affairs, Tactical Operations, Detective, and Regional Organized Crime & Narcotics), and the Operations Branch consists of the Traffic Division, Transit, and five Patrol Precincts. In the Operations Branch, an assistant chief oversees the five precincts, while each precinct has one commander.

Patrol Geographic and Shift Structure

PPB patrol spans five precincts (i.e., Central, North, Northeast, East, and Southeast) with each precinct operating out of a police substation. Compared to the two large police agencies (i.e., CPD and CMPD), PPB is less spatially differentiated. Each precinct is geographically broken down into districts, which are further broken down into grids. The commander in each precinct has three lieutenants (e.g., morning, afternoon, and night), each lieutenant has four sergeants, and each sergeant has between six and 10 officers under his/her command. Patrol officers are assigned to precincts. However, only approximately two-thirds of patrol officers are assigned to specific districts within these precincts. The rest of the patrol officers are categorized as "utility" and may be assigned to any district on an as-needed basis.

PPB patrol operates on three shifts (day, afternoon, and night), with no swing (or overlapping) shift. The day shift runs from 0700–1700; the afternoon shift runs from 1600–0200; and the night shift runs from 2200–0800. Patrol shifts are 10 hours in duration, and officers work four days a week. Roll calls are conducted at each precinct at the start of each shift.

Promotional Structure

After five to seven years of working as a patrol officer, officers reach their top pay level and can work to be promoted to one of three positions, each of which is equal pay (i.e., 15 percent above the top patrol officer pay): detective (civil service), sergeant (civil service), and criminalist (civil service). After 12 to 13 total years in the Bureau, detectives and sergeants can take the lieutenant's exam, which is also a civil service position (criminalists are not eligible for any further promotions). Lieutenants can become captains (civil service) and some captains (13 at the time of the study in the Bureau) can be appointed to commander (eight at the time of the study in the Bureau), although they are technically the same in rank. Finally, the three assistant chiefs and the chief of police are appointed positions.

Specialized Units

Each of the five precincts has one allocated detective-based Neighborhood Response Team (NRT), whose officers do not respond to 911 calls and work in plain clothes. NRTs are variable among precincts in the sense that they use a Problem-Oriented Policing (POP; Goldstein, 1990) approach to address pressing crime problems. In addition, several other units operate out of PPB. The K-9 Unit is housed in the Southeast Precinct (deployed citywide as needed), while Mounted Patrol is housed in the Central Precinct, and Special Emergency Reaction Team (SERT), Hostage Negotiations Team (HNT), and Explosives Disposal Unit (EDU) are all situated within the Tactical Operations Division. Again, compared to the previous large police organizations, PPB would be regarded as less functionally differentiated.

Unions/Collective Bargaining

There are two unions with collective bargaining powers. The Portland Police Association represents patrol officers, sergeants, detectives, and criminalists. According to PPB officials, this union is very strong, which is similar to CPD (but not CMPD). The Portland Police Commanding Officers Association (PPCOA) represents the lieutenants, captains, and commanders.

Supervisory Oversight for Use of Force Documentation and Complaints

Every officer who uses force (i.e., everything above handcuffing/simple restraint) must complete a use of force report. Primary officers involved in the incident are required to fill out all mandatory reports and also write a narrative account of their actions in separate custody/incident reports.

Supervisors are not required to go to the scene of every use of force incident. Instead, supervisors are directed to respond to the scene in instances where a subject has been hit by a less lethal impact weapon or in instances where an officer has negligently or unintentionally discharged the Taser®. As such, officers are required to notify supervisors immediately whenever the baton, chemical spray, Taser®, or less lethal weapons are deployed on a subject. In these cases, supervisors are supposed to document any injuries in an inter-office memorandum, most often an after-action report, which are narratives that describe and evaluate a police action. Although supervisors are not required to go to the scene in all instances, they are responsible for reviewing every use of force report written by their officers. After supervisory review, they are sent to the Records Division for electronic entry.

A Use of Force Review Board (UFRB) reviews the following incidents: officer-involved shootings, serious injury to a subject that requires hospitalization, in-custody deaths, less lethal incidents that are recommended to be out of policy, and any discretionary incidents referred by the chief or branch chiefs. The UFRB then determines whether the use of force was within or out of policy. It may also make recommendations regarding the quality of investigations, the findings of investigations, the level of discipline, and may also suggest issues that address training or policy.

The UFRB is composed of nine voting members and three non-voting members, three branch chiefs (the Services Branch chief is the chair), one non-involved responding unit (RU) manager, RU manager of the officer under review, two peer members of similar rank to the officer under review, two citizen members, Review Board coordinator (non-voting), representative from Human Resources (non-voting), representative from City Attorney's Office (non-voting).

The Detectives Division conducts the initial investigation to determine if criminal charges are to be filed and if any grand jury hearings are necessary. If not, then the case is forwarded to IA and the Training Division for review and to further investigate if the officer's conduct was in or out of policy. These investigations are sent to the officer's RU manager who reviews the case, makes a finding, makes a recommendation for discipline (if the finding is sustained), and forwards the results to the branch chief. If the branch chief concurs then the case goes to UFRB for review. Decisions from the case are reviewed by the chief and the mayor has the final authority.

Complaints against PPB officers are classified as citizen (external), departmental (internal), or tort claims. Following investigation (if applicable, see process below), findings are classified as: justified within policy, justified out of policy, justified tactical improvement needed, not justified/not within policy. Citizen complaints begin in the Independent Police Review (IPR) division, an external entity housed in the city auditor's office. The IPR has five primary responsibilities: receive citizen complaints, monitor complaint investigations conducted by IA, report on complaint and investigation activities, report on policy and investigation issues involving officer-involved shootings and in-custody deaths, and coordinate the complaint appeals process with the Citizen Review Committee (CRC) and the city council.

After IPR receives a citizen complaint, it is reviewed for merit. Copies of complaints that are dismissed at this stage are sent to IA for informational purposes only, and a letter to the complainant is sent outlining the reasons for dismissal. Complaints that are deemed to have merit by IPR are then forwarded to IA. IPR can instruct IA in one of three ways: to refer the complaint to IA for investigation, request that IA investigate with IPR involvement, or request that IPR will conduct the investigation with IA involvement.

Citizen complaints referred to IA can then be dismissed, investigated, conducted as an inquiry, or treated as a service complaint. Inquiries are conducted at the precinct level. If a citizen complaint is investigated by IA, the results are forwarded to the commanding officer of the officer named in the complaint. IA does not make any findings; they simply serve as an investigating body. The commanding officer makes the first report of findings and may decide to sustain or not sustain the complaint. The assistant chief of Operations either concurs or controverts with the commanding officer's findings. At this point, no recommendations for discipline are made.

If the complaint is not sustained, then IA notifies IPR and provides the reason for the decision (e.g., insufficient evidence, exonerated, or unfounded). IPR then informs the complainant of the decision and notifies him or her of any appeals processes that might be relevant. If the complaint is sustained then a recommendation is made and sent to personnel, review committees, and the chief of police. The chief of police reviews the recommendation, and if he/she concurs with the decision, the Personnel Division notifies the officer and IA notifies IPR, which is then responsible for notifying the complainant of the decision. If the commanding officer and the assistant chief controvert then the case goes to the appropriate review board (e.g., Performance or Use of Force) that makes the recommendation. If either IA or IPR disagrees with the commanding officer and assistant chief's decision, then the case will also go before the appropriate review board. Few cases, however, are ever controverted. According to officials at IPR, disagreements tend to be handled more informally where discussion goes back and forth between the dissenting party and the commanding officer.

Results of the complaint process then go back to the IPR division for storage. If the officer disagrees with a sustained complaint, he/she can also file an appeal with IPR, which will be directed to CRC. If a citizen files an appeal that cannot be resolved by the CRC then the decision is made by the City Council (but this is rare). Interestingly, IPR officials have noted that in several years the department has never sustained a use of force complaint. Instead, the department reports that the use of force was within policy, but the officer's performance was deficient and so the case technically becomes a performance case rather than a use of force case.

The Performance Review Board (PRB) has numerous review functions: sustained findings in investigations that propose suspension without pay as discipline; controverted findings in investigations; IPR returns for reconsideration; Equal Employment Opportunity investigations; recommendations regarding the quality of investigations, the findings of investigations, and the level of discipline; and the PRB may also suggest issues that address training or policy. The PRB is composed of six voting members and three non-voting members: three branch chiefs with the Services Branch chief serving as the chair, one peer member of rank similar to that of the officer under review, one citizen selected from a pre-approved pool of volunteers, the RU manager of the officer under review, Review Board coordinator (non-voting), a representative from Human Resources (non-voting), and a representative from the City Attorney's Office (non-voting).

The PRB process usually begins as a result of a citizen or bureau initiated complaint, typically complaints of excessive physical force. At the PRB meeting the RU manager presents the facts of the case. If the PRB votes to sustain a finding, a recommendation for the level of discipline is made. Both the majority and minority opinions of the voting members are sent to the chief of police for review. Ultimately, the finding and recommended discipline in a sustained case is the chief's decision. Everything the PRB does is a recommendation to the chief, who will determine the course of action and then return the case to the PRB for processing.

Regarding discipline of complaints, actions that are considered less than suspension, such as a Letter of Expectation, Command Counseling, or a Letter of Reprimand are the responsibilities of the RU manager for implementation. If there is a suspension or more severe form of discipline, the case goes before the review boards. In terms of tracking problematic behavior, agency contacts indicated that the Early Warning (EW) system was not yet in place during the study period, while IPR officials implied that it was in place, but not used.

Albuquerque (New Mexico) Police Department

The Albuquerque Police Department (APD), another one of our mid-sized police agencies, employs 986 sworn personnel, 456 of which are assigned to street level patrol. Compared to PPB, APD has virtually the same number of sworn employees, although they have a higher percentage (46) patrolling the street. In terms of police per 1,000 citizens, APD has 1.92, which is the most of the three mid-sized police departments.

Administrative Structure

The administrative structure of APD, in terms of functional differentiation, is slightly less specialized than that of PPB. The Chief's Office houses four divisions (Fiscal, Planning & Policy, Strategic Support, and Internal Affairs), a Public Information Officer (PIO), an Education Coordinator, a Legal Advisor, and an Executive Assistant. Beneath the chief are four primary Bureaus, with a number of divisions within each. The Administrative Bureau contains four divisions (Support Services, Professional Standards, Communications, and Human Resources). There are three divisions located within the Investigative Bureau (Special Investigations, Criminal Investigations, and Property Crimes). The Field Services Bureau consists of Community Services, the Behavioral Science Division, and five patrol Area Commands. The Investigative, Administrative, and Field Services Bureaus are each commanded by a deputy chief, while the Support Services Bureau is headed by an executive director. A deputy chief oversees the five patrol area commands, while each individual area command is led by a captain (called an area commander).

Patrol Geographic and Shift Structure

APD patrol spans five area commands (Foothills Area, Northeast Area, Southeast Area, Valley Area, and Westside Area), with each operating out of a police substation. This degree of spatial differentiation is identical to that of

PPB. Each Area Command is organized by districts and further broken down into patrol beats. A captain is in charge of leading each of the five command areas, which also have three lieutenants assigned to them (day, swing, and graveyard shift). Each lieutenant has, on average, three to four sergeants who operate a team, and each team has on average of seven to 13 officers assigned. These teams are often designated by the days of the week that officers work. At the beginning of the year, officers place a bid on the area and shift that they want to be assigned. Although APD officers are assigned to a given area command and shift, they are not always assigned to a specific beat. Due to staffing challenges, supervisors cannot always fill every beat so they assign on an as-needed basis.

APD patrol operates on four shifts (day, swing, graveyard, and split). The day shift runs from 0700–1700, the swing shift runs from 1400–2400, the graveyard shift runs from 2200–0800, and the split shift runs from 1700–0300. Shifts are 10 hours in duration and officers work four days a week. Roll call briefings are conducted at each area command substation.

Promotional Structure

Following the police academy, officers are considered patrol officers 2nd Class. Following a one-year probationary period, officers become patrol officers 1st Class. Officers can be promoted to sergeant and then lieutenant after taking a city administered exam. Those with the highest exam grade scores are hired for the position. The chief of police recently developed a process to promote lieutenants to captains. Captains can be moved or demoted, but not fired. The four deputy chiefs and the chief are appointed positions.

Specialized Units

In addition to patrol, APD has a number of specialized units that are organized within the Investigative and Services Bureaus. In the Investigative Bureau, there is a Career Criminal Section which houses the Intelligence, Gangs, Vice, Crisis Intervention, and Crisis Negotiation Units; a Narcotics Section; a Violent Crimes Section which houses the Sex Crimes, Armed Robbery, and Homicide Units; and Property Crimes Section which houses the White Collar Crime, Auto Theft, and Burglary Units. In the Support Services Bureau, there is a Tactical Section which houses the Emergency Response Unit, K-9 Unit, and the SWAT Teams; a Traffic Section which houses the Traffic Enforcement Teams and DUI Unit; and a Tactical Support Section which houses the Air Support and Horse Mounted Patrol Units.

Unions/Collective Bargaining

The department has one primary union, the Albuquerque Police Officer Association (APOA), which officers are required to join. There are two membership options: a "basic" membership or one that also includes litigation representation. The department also has a Chicano Police Officers Association (CPOA). Ranks of captains and above are not protected by the union.

Supervisory Oversight for Use of Force Documentation and Complaints

Every APD officer who uses force (i.e., everything above handcuffing/simple restraint) must complete a use of force report bubblesheet (e.g., a form that resembles a scantron) in addition to an incident report. Supervisors are responsible for ensuring that use of force bubblesheets are filed when officers use force, but they are not required to go to the scene. If an officer does not fill out the report, it is the responsibility of the supervisor to do so. It is also the responsibility of the supervisor to review all subordinate officers' use of force bubblesheet forms. The supervisor must sign the form and note whether the force used was appropriate, or if an investigation is warranted. According to several department and city officials, in recent years, officers' use of force reporting was somewhat sporadic due to a broader organizational perception that filling them out was not important and that supervisors had never needed to ensure that they were filled out. When supervisors began to be held accountable for use of force reporting, and the Independent Review Office (IRO) began automatically requesting these forms when a complaint of excessive force was made, use of force reporting improved. However, by several accounts, reporting of force was still somewhat of a concern, although the extent or magnitude of such is unknown. Such a concern was not shared by any of the other six agencies.

Copies of all use of force bubblesheets and accompanying incident reports are submitted to the Operations Review lieutenant within 72 hours of the incident. The Operations Review lieutenant then distributes the reports to Internal Affairs (IA), Risk Management, the Legal Department, Tactical Teams, and the Training Academy when appropriate. The lieutenant ensures that the report is reviewed by the Legal Department and forwarded to IA. Finally, it is the commander's responsibility to ensure that all supervisors and subordinates conform to the policy and that all reports are submitted to the appropriate units. All use of force data are electronically stored and housed with IA.

Complaints against officers are classified as citizen (external), departmental (internal), or tort claims. Following investigation (if applicable, see process below), findings are classified as: sustained (i.e., the allegation is supported by sufficient proof), not sustained (i.e., the evidence is not sufficient to prove or disprove the allegation), unfounded (i.e., the allegation is false or otherwise not based on valid facts), exonerated (i.e., the incident that occurred or was complained against was lawful and proper), or misconduct not based on the original complaint (i.e., the evidence supports the action or infractions discovered during the investigation of a complaint that may be sustained, not sustained, unfounded, or exonerated).

The city's Independent Review Office (IRO) (created from a 1999 city ordinance) receives all citizen complaints. The IRO office is headed by an IRO officer who is a contract employee hired by the mayor. The office also has three investigators who are city employees. In early years, the IRO investigated approximately 60 percent of use of force complaints and assigned the other 40 percent to IA. At the time of the study, IRO investigated all complaints involving excessive force claims. Also, all complaints involving officers of the lieutenant rank or higher are automatically sent to the IRO for investigation.

IRO decides whether they will investigate or assign the complaint to IA. If IRO takes a case, it is assigned to one of three IRO investigators. A letter is sent to the complainant, as well as the alleged officer. APD mandates that only those complaints signed by complainant can be investigated. The investigator separately interviews both the complainant and the officer. IRO looks for violations of policy by the officer and makes a finding.

The investigation and findings are then sent to the IRO officer for review. The IRO officer can concur or change the finding. The results of the case are then sent to IA for review.

IA forwards the results to the appropriate area command captain for review. Results are then sent to the deputy chief and chief for review. If all parties agree, then the case proceeds as "found." APD allocates all of the disciplinary responsibilities against officers to the chief of police. If the chief disagrees, he/she holds a non-concurrence meeting to discuss further. Normally this results in a conclusion. If no conclusion can be reached, then the case goes to the Police Oversight Commission (POC) for finding.

The POC is composed of nine community members—one member per city council district. To be on the commission, individuals must be community members with no law enforcement experience, but they are required to conduct two ride-alongs per year with APD as well as go through the Firearms Training Simulator (FATS) at the academy each year. Members must also receive civil rights training. The POC also oversees investigation of citizen complaints and monitors investigations of IA, reviews work of the IRO, and reviews complaints when the chief or IRO officer disagrees with IRO findings. Both the chief of police and POC findings go into officers' retention cards. The citizen may appeal to POC and appear at the monthly POC meeting. POC will then make a finding. One last final appeal can be made to the city's chief administrative officer.

In addition to complaint investigations, the IRO reviews and monitors IA cases and discusses these cases with the department, and makes policy and training recommendations to the POC and APD (e.g., if IRO finds that a policy is improper in some way they can sustain a complaint against the department rather than an individual). The mediation process is not used for use of force complaints. Discipline is determined by a "Chart of Sanctions" that considers the severity of the current offense and disciplinary record of the officer. Officers can appeal disciplinary sanctions to the city's chief administrative officer.

APD utilizes an Early Warning (EW) system to monitor officer behavior. Officers enter the EW system if they are involved in five qualifying incidents in a 12-month time period. Qualifying incidents include: use of force incidents; citizen complaints, regardless of findings; internal investigations, regardless of findings; firearm discharge; missed court; range training, or physical assessment; preventable police vehicle accidents; tort claims—litigation, civil law suits. Once the threshold for the EW system has been met, information is forwarded to the officer's division head, who is responsible for holding a face-to-face meeting and notifying IA of the meeting's outcome. Potential outcomes may include: training, employee assistance programs, and other departmental resources. Emphasis of the APD's EW system is training and counseling as opposed to punishment oriented. If an officer is involved in 10 or more qualifying incidents in a 12-month time period, s/he is referred to the department's Behavioral Science Division. The EW system has a review panel, which consists of: deputy chief of Administration, officer's area commander, IA unit commander (e.g., EW system coordinator), Selection and Training commander, a Behavioral Sciences Division representative, a preferred peer of the officer, and a union representative. This panel may be called upon to convene to consider the need to provide corrective action, if any, for employees identified in the EW system. All of EW system records are housed with IA.

Colorado Springs (Colorado) Police Department

The Colorado Springs Police Department (CSPD), our third mid-sized agency, employs 669 sworn personnel. The 317 sworn personnel assigned to street-level patrol functions is proportionally (47 percent) similar to APD. Of all research sites, CSPD has the fewest number of officers per 1,000 citizens (1.79).

Administrative Structure

CSPD has three primary bureaus that are directed by the Chief's Office: the Patrol Bureau, Operations Support Bureau, and the Office of Professional Standards. The Patrol Bureau consists of the four Patrol Divisions (i.e., precincts) and is overseen by a deputy chief. The Operations Support Bureau is also overseen by a deputy chief and contains four divisions: Investigations, Vice Narcotics and Intelligence (VNI), Central Support Services, and Central Management Services. The Office of Professional Standards is overseen by a commander and contains Internal Affairs, the Public Information Office, the Training Academy, and Human Resources. Of all three mid-sized agencies, CSPD is the least functionally differentiated.

Patrol Geographic and Shift Structure

Patrol functions are dispersed across four patrol divisions (Falcon, Gold Hill, Sand Creek, and Stetson Hills). Each division operates out of a police substation. This degree of spatial differentiation is shared by the other two mid-sized agencies. Each division is also broken down into sectors. At the beginning of the year, officers are assigned to divisions and shift times based upon their selections/preferences. Although officers are assigned to a given division and shift for the year, they are often not permanently assigned to sectors, which are filled on a rotating basis based on allocation needs for the shift.

CSPD operates on three shifts (day, middle, and night), which are staffed according to a computerized software workload analyzer. The day and middle shifts have two overlapping start times (day 0600 and 0900, middle 1400 and 1700) while the night shift starts at 2100. Shifts are 10 hours in duration, and officers work four days a week. Debriefings as part of roll call are conducted at each area command substation.

Promotional Structure

The promotion process to sergeant or lieutenant begins with an exam. After completion of the exam, officers are placed in bands (A, B, or C) based upon their exam score. When a sergeant or lieutenant position opens up, the chief of police selects an officer for the position from band A. Exam scores and results are valid for two years. The chief appoints promotions to the rank of division commander and deputy chief.

Specialized Units

The department has a number of specialized units, many of which are operated out of the Operations Support Bureau. The Investigations Division within the Operations Support Bureau contains a Major Crimes Unit which focuses on homicide, sex crimes, robbery, and juvenile crimes as well as a Special Services Unit which focuses on computer and financial crimes. CSPD's VNI Division focuses on vice, narcotics, and intelligence. The Central Division within the Operations Bureau houses the K-9 Unit, Air Support Unit, Airport Police, and the Tactical Enforcement Unit.

In addition to the specialized units housed within the Operations Support Bureau, some specialized units are also housed within each patrol division. For example, each patrol division houses a traffic unit as well as DUI specialists, School Resource Officers, and Neighborhood Policing Units. CSPD also recently added Community Impact (COMMIT) teams to target gun, gang, and drug problems within the city. There are four COMMIT teams (one for each patrol division), each of which contains 10 officers and one sergeant.

Unions/Collective Bargaining

The department is not unionized and is not allowed to collectively bargain due to the city charter. This is an organizational feature similar to the Charlotte-Mecklenburg and Fort Wayne Police Departments.

Supervisory Oversight for Use of Force Documentation and Complaints

Every officer who uses force (i.e., everything above handcuffing/simple restraint) must complete a use of force report (called a Response To Aggression report or RTA). As part of the policy, supervisors are required to respond to the scene; however, pending extreme cases involving injury or some other circumstance a supervisor believes warrants, the supervisor does not interview officers, witnesses, or the suspect. Rather, s/he is just present to oversee the reporting process.

Once completed, use of force forms are sent to an administrative sergeant who reviews each form, makes a copy, and puts it in the officer's file. The original form then goes to the shift/section lieutenant for review, then division commander reviews, and finally to the Professional Standards/Inspections Unit. Summary data from the force report (i.e., a synopsis of the event) are also stored electronically within the department. The data are compiled quarterly and sent to the training academy to be reviewed where trends are identified to determine if the uses of force being reported are preventable or non-preventable.

Complaints against officers are classified as citizen initiated (e.g., external), department initiated (e.g., internal), or supervisor initiated (e.g., supervisory). An internal complaint includes allegations such as showing up late for work, while a supervisory complaint includes performance-related allegations. Following an investigation (if applicable, see process below), findings are classified as: not a policy violation (e.g., invalid), unfounded, not sustained, exonerated, sustained, misconduct not based on complaint (i.e., a supervisor discovers a sustained policy violation unrelated to the complainant's original allegation, or closed by mediation).

IA or supervisors/commanding officers can accept complaints. It is the responsibility of the person receiving the complaint to conduct a "preliminary inquiry" and complete a complaint receipt form. Based upon the preliminary inquiry, a complaint warranting an investigation is categorized as either a Level I or Level II investigation. Level I investigations are conducted by supervisors within the officer's division. Level II investigations are conducted by IA. The primary differences between a Level I and a Level II investigation include: seriousness of the allegation or discipline (more serious allegations or resulting discipline would constitute a Level II investigation), prior behavior of the officer (if a pattern of behavior is identified, a Level II investigation may be initiated, even if the current alleged charge is less severe), and who conducts the investigation.

Although either IA or the division can conduct either type of investigation, IA investigates Level II cases and the division investigates both Level I and Level II cases. For example, allegations involving misuse of force may be investigated as a Level I or a Level II. It is the amount of force used and the past behavior of the officer that would be the deciding factors. A force case may initially start as a Level I investigation but then move to a Level II. In essence, command officers in the divisions are responsible for investigating a large portion of complaints. How a case is investigated is based on a judgment call made either at the division or IA. Of particular note, IA investigates all allegations of "excessive force" and all instances where a firearm was discharged. In Level I cases, notification of the results to the complainant is made by the supervisor of the alleged officer; in Level II cases notification of results is made by IA.

Disciplinary actions against officers include both informal (training or verbal counseling) and formal (written reprimand, individual performance plan, suspension, demotion in rank or grade, termination or dismissal from the department) options. Disciplinary actions for Level I investigations can only include training or verbal counseling. All recommended disciplinary actions are reviewed by the officer's chain of command: sergeant/immediate supervisor, lieutenant/reviewing supervisor, division commander, deputy chief, and chief of police. The chief of police has the final say on disciplinary action. If a complaint is sustained and disciplinary action greater than a written reprimand is handed down, the officer can accept the disciplinary action or appeal by requesting a board of rights to be formed or requesting the case be reviewed by a deputy chief not in the officer's chain of command.

CSPD utilizes an early warning system referred to as the Early Intervention Program (EIP). An EIP report is generated for officers in one of two ways depending on an officer's behavior over a six- or 12-month time period. The six-month criteria is as follows: officer involved in three or more use of force incidents, officer is the subject of two or more service-related citizen complaints (Level I and/or Level II) that have either been disposed as sustained or not sustained, officer involved in two or more on-duty vehicle accidents, no matter who is at fault, officer involved in two or more deadly force and/or accidental discharge of a firearm incidents. The 12-month criteria is as follows: officer involved in four or more use of force incidents, officer is the subject of four or more service-related citizen complaints (Level I and/or Level II) that have either been disposed as sustained or not sustained, officer involved in three or more on-duty vehicle accidents, no matter who is at fault, officer involved in three or more deadly force incidents during career. Police officials note that a majority of EIP reports come from use of force incidents.

For each EIP generated, a field sergeant evaluates the incidents involved and discusses them with the officer, lieutenant, and division commander. EIP was not implemented to be disciplinary, but could be punishment oriented (e.g., if a trend is uncovered). Once officers are identified by EIP it is hard for them to get out of review because the process has a cumulative effect. The department also has an Employee Activity Program (EAP), a completely confidential program, which develops a performance improvement plan outlining what needs to be done as a result of the trends noticed. However, this program is rarely used—only two cases during the two year study period.

Fort Wayne (Indiana) Police Department

The Fort Wayne Police Department (FWPD) is one of our two smaller agencies with 457 sworn officers. In terms of officers assigned to patrol, FWPD deploys roughly half of their sworn personnel (221) to such positions. FWPD, like that of PPB, has 1.84 police per 1,000 residents, which places them in a tie for the second fewest of the seven agencies.

Administrative Structure

For a smaller police department, FWPD is fairly functionally differentiated, with a number of specialized units located among six primary divisions of operation. Within the Chief's Office are the Office of Professional Standards (that houses Internal Affairs), Information Systems and Technology, Fiscal Affairs, The Police Academy, Neighborhood Code Enforcement, and the Neighborhood Response Team. At the bottom of the organizational chart lie the six divisions of operation. Four of the divisions (Northwest Division 1, Northeast Division 2, Southwest Division 3, and Southeast Division 4) are responsible for patrol functions, while a fifth (Investigative Support Division) handles investigative responsibilities. Each of these divisions is overseen by a deputy chief (one for each division). The final division is Information Systems, which handles the Communications Center and Records Section, and is headed by a director.

Patrol Geographic and Shift Structure

FWPD's patrol is dispersed among four quadrants (Northeast, Northwest, Southeast, and Southwest). Patrol quadrants are further broken down into districts and then sectors. Each quadrant is led by a captain, and there is a captain assigned to oversee each shift covering all quadrants. Across the quadrants, there are also lieutenants (a merit position) who serve an administrative function, and sergeants who are the primary shift supervisors for officers on the street. FWPD is somewhat unique in that they have more captains than lieutenants (i.e., top heavy). At the time of the study there were 14 captains, but far fewer lieutenants. Patrol officers are assigned to a specific district and shift within each quadrant. Officers can make unlimited bids for assignments whenever an opening emerges. Bid assignments in Fort Wayne, like many police organizations, are based on seniority.

The department operates on three shifts (A, B, and C). The A shift runs from 0600 to 1430, B shift runs from 1400 to 2230, and C shift runs from 2200 to 0630. Shifts are 8.5 hours in duration, and officers work a schedule of four days on and two days off. Fort Wayne is different from the other six agencies in that they do not use a traditional roll call system. Rather, officers have take-home cars and check in for their shift using their car computer terminal. Thus, officers do not typically go to their respective quadrants for a pre-shift briefing, but begin their tours of duty in their respective district.

Promotional Structure

Officers are on probationary status for the first year. After the first year, officers are at the rank of patrol. Similar to our other agencies, the ranks of sergeant and lieutenant are merit positions within the department. The mayor makes the appointments to the ranks of captain, deputy chief, assistant chief, and chief of police.

Specialized Units

The department has a number of specialized units that operate primarily out of specific Patrol Quadrants or the Investigations Division. For example, Emergency Services (i.e., SWAT), Special Events, and HIT/SKIP operate out of the Northwest Quadrant. The Critical Incident Team operates out of the Northeast Quadrant. The K-9 Unit operates out of the Southwest Quadrant. The School Child Safety Program and Crime Prevention operate out of the Southwest Quadrant. The Crime Analysis Unit and the Victim Assistance Program are housed in the Investigations Division.

Unions/Collective Bargaining

Among FWPD officers, there are two union options. The PBA is primarily a union for patrol officers, and the FOP is a union primarily for sergeants and lieutenants; however, patrol officers may also join.

Supervisory Oversight for Use of Force Documentation and Complaints

Every officer who uses force (i.e., any force type) is required to fill out a use of force report form in addition to an incident report. After officers fill out use of force report forms, a sergeant reviews and signs off on them. Supervisors are not required to go to the scene when force is used. The use of force report form is then attached to the incident report and sent to the Office of Professional Standards. The Office of Professional Standards, IA, and the Training Center all maintain copies of the force reports. IA uses the force reports to aid in the investigation of excessive force complaints, as well as to compile an annual review of use of force incidents that is included in the department's annual report. The Training Center also reviews force reports to ensure that they are being filled out properly using the appropriate language. The training instructor also determines whether certain techniques taught to officers are ineffective. An example of the "sidekick" was given by trainers where upon review it was found that this technique was ineffective. As a result, the sidekick was eliminated as a use of force technique.

Complaints against officers are classified as citizen (external), departmental (internal), or tort claims (as well as Equal Employment Opportunity Claim (EEOC)). Following investigation (if applicable, see process below), findings are classified as: sustained, not sustained, unfounded, or exonerated. IA is charged with investigating complaints. In determining findings, IA does not only look at whether policy was violated, but also looks at the totality of circumstances surrounding the allegation. In order for a complaint to be investigated, according to FWPD policy, it must be signed by the complainant(s).

Once a complaint is made, IA decides whether to investigate or reject the claim. All complaints alleging excessive use of force must be investigated by IA. If a complaint is rejected, a letter is sent to the complainant outlining the reason for the rejection. These complaints and letters are filed at IA. If a complaint is investigated, a 48-hour notice is sent to the officer, complainant, and witnesses providing information and request for interviews. IA conducts interviews, reviews the case, and makes a recommendation for findings and discipline. The assistant chief reviews the investigation with the recommendation and can either concur with findings or make an alternative suggestion. If the assistant chief concurs with the findings, the most severe discipline that can be imposed is a five-day suspension. Any disciplinary action greater than a five-day suspension must be presented to the Board of Public Safety, which reviews such suspension recommendations as well as instances where a citizen appeals the department's findings.

The internal complaint process is similar. Officers can fill out an Allegation of Misconduct form, which is circulated up through the chain of command to the assistant chief and IA. In the event that an internal complaint is against an officer's supervisor, the chain of command can be bypassed and the form can be sent straight to the assistant chief. Minor forms of misconduct do not circulate to IA until a more serious threshold has been crossed. For example, officer tardiness will not go to IA until the fourth occurrence. Also minor forms of misconduct or vehicle accidents will not compound the disciplinary actions for other forms of policy violations or allegations of misconduct.

The city of Fort Wayne also institutes a three-member Board of Public Safety (i.e., form of civilian oversight) composed of citizen volunteers who are appointed by the mayor. The board's primary purpose is to review the department's disciplinary and hiring practices as well as resignations from the department. Although the board does not review all citizen complaint investigations, they can review cases and make findings for cases involving disciplinary action greater than a five-day suspension or for cases involving citizen appeals.

Discipline against officers is based on a progressive system where penalties are classified from Class A (most severe) to Class F (least severe). Penalties within each class are also based on the number of officer offenses. The penalty for the use of excessive force is categorized as a Class C penalty with punishment for the first offense being a five-day suspension and third offense being a determinate suspension or dismissal. However, per FWPD's rules and regulations, "if in the determination of the chief of police or his designee, the force used was not excessive but unreasonable, the penalty will be reduced to a Class E offense." Like that of the Portland Police Bureau, FWPD does not have a mechanism in place to track potentially problematic officer behavior (i.e., Early Warning or Early Intervention systems).

Knoxville (Tennessee) Police Department

The Knoxville Police Department (KPD) has the fewest number of sworn personnel (382) of all study sites, 176 (42 percent) of which are assigned to street patrol. While KPD is categorized as one of our smaller sites, their 2.09 officers per 1,000 Knoxville residents ranks third, behind our two largest agencies (i.e., Columbus Police Department and Charlotte-Mecklenburg Police Department).

Administrative Structure

KPD's organizational structure, and functional differentiation, resembles that of the Portland Police Bureau. The Chief's Office houses an Executive Staff Officer, a Public Information Officer, and an Office of Professional Standards (which includes Internal Affairs, Inspections, and Accreditation). There are four main operational divisions (i.e., Patrol, Criminal Investigation, Support Services, and Management Support), with a deputy chief assigned to each division. The Patrol Division includes: Special Operations, East District, West District, Central Business District, and Traffic. The Criminal Investigation Division includes: Family Services, Forensics, Intelligence, Crimes Against Persons, Crimes Against Property, and Organized Crime. The Support Services Division includes: Training, Property and Evidence, Safety Education,

Records, and Communications. The Management Support Division includes: Budget, Accreditation, Information Services, Planning, Personnel, and Building Services.

Patrol Geographic and Shift Structure

KPD's patrol operations span two districts (East and West). Across each district there are seven squads (A–G). Patrol officers are assigned to a specific district and squad (and beat) within each of these districts. A captain heads each of the two districts. In the East District there are approximately 11 officers, two sergeants and one lieutenant per squad. In the West District there are approximately nine officers, two sergeants and one lieutenant per squad.

KPD operates on five shifts. The three primary shifts are 9.5 hours long with respective start times of 0630, 1400, and 2130. Officers on squads A, B, C, D, and E cover these three shifts. Officers work six days on and four days off, rotating every 10 days across the three shifts. The remaining two shifts are midwatch day (start time of 1000) and midwatch night (start time of 1800) shifts that are 10 hours in duration. Officers from Squads F and G work these shifts for four days on and three days off. Both midwatch squads are required to work on Friday. Officers on these two shifts rotate every 28 days. Roll calls are conducted at each of the two districts before each shift.

Promotional Structure

Based on seniority, there are five levels of the patrol rank. The process for promotions in rank to sergeant, lieutenant, and captain is standardized, and based on civil service criteria. Deputy chiefs and higher are appointed positions, and the only ranks that require a four-year college degree. For captains and lieutenants "some" college is required. The promotional process generally includes the following elements: a standardized written test, a training and education evaluation, an in-basket exam, an outside oral interview, an "insight" interview, and an examination of all annual reports, work history, complaints, training, and use of force. Across all promotions, the top five people are evaluated for every one opening. Candidates are hierarchically ranked, based on the above criteria, and scores are averaged.

Specialized Units

KPD has a number of specialized units that operate primarily out of the Critical Incident component of the Special Operations section of the Patrol

Division, which include: Explosive Ordinance Disposal Detail (EOD), Special Operation Squad (SOS), Hostage Negotiation Unit, Weapons of Mass Destruction Unit (WMD), Search and Recovery Unit (SAR), and Marine Unit. Other specialized units within the Patrol Division include: K-9 Unit, Motorcycle Unit, and the Teleserve Unit.

Unions/Collective Bargaining

Tennessee is a "right to work" state, so there are no unions. Police officers may choose to belong "locally" to one of two national organizations—FOP and/or PBA. These organizations are available to officers of all ranks. The PBA is generally reserved for patrol officers, and the FOP is primarily for sergeants and lieutenants; however patrol officers may also join. Both groups meet regularly with the chief of police to discuss police issues.

Supervisory Oversight for Use of Force Documentation and Complaints

Officers are required to fill out a use of force report form at level two (empty hand soft, baton soft, contact controls, direction controls) and above of a five level policy or if a suspect has (or complains) of an injury. Once force forms are filled out, they are given to sergeants for their review. Informally, the department likes to have the supervisor present (not on scene) when the officer is filling out the report to reduce errors in reporting. KPD is unique, compared to the other six departments, in that they videotape all police incidents that occur in view of the patrol car, and they audio record all police-citizen interactions. Both of these recordings (especially the audio) are consulted when use of force documentation is done by the officer. Informally, the department encourages supervisors to go to the scene in Taser® cases, although it is not explicitly in the policy. Supervisors are officially required to go the scenes in which deadly force is used by an officer.

Once a force report form is filled out it goes up the officer's chain of command. Per the form, a signature is required for immediate supervisor (who reviews the audio and video recording), a lieutenant, and a captain. A formal review of the form is also conducted by IA. Reports are also reviewed by the deputy chief of Patrol, the chief of police, and Training. All hard copies of use of force reports are stored with IA.

Complaints against officers originate from either external (from citizens and through civilian oversight—Public Advisory and Review Committee (PARC)) or internal (from the chief and command staff) sources. KPD categorizes complaints as "referrals" (less serious in nature and do not result in a formal IA investigation) and "formal investigations" (more serious in nature). Formal investigations are the only complaints that are given a unit case number and are notarized once received. Following investigations (i.e., both referrals and formal), a complaint may be classified as: 1st degree – sustained, 2nd degree – not sustained, 3rd degree – exonerated, 4th degree – unfounded, and 5th degree – police failure "exonerated."

Investigating supervisors, with the approval of a district or unit commander, determine if a complaint will be a "referral," while IA, with the approval of the chief of police and the Legal Department, determine "formal investigations." All complaints are filtered through IA, which enables them to monitor, as a check and balance system, the referral investigations. Also, all complaints, whoever receives them, have to be sent to IA, via the referral action form, within 72 hours of receiving the complaint. Complainants are required to fill out the first part of the referral action form. The complainant is immediately informed, in writing, that the complaint was received by IA, and who is handling the investigation.

Referrals (both internal and external) (e.g., rudeness, discourtesy, failure to investigate, etc.) are referred to the officer's immediate supervisor, who is in charge of investigating the complaint. This usually starts with reviewing audio/video tapes and interviewing the officer. The investigating supervisor then disposes of the referral in one of the five ways listed above (1st–5th degree). If sustained, the supervisor documents proper punishment (usually some counseling or training). This decision has to be done (and forwarded to IA) within 15 working days of when the supervisor received the notice from IA.

Formal Investigations are more serious allegations and are assigned a unit case number by IA, who conducts the investigations against the police department and all city employees. The investigatory process begins by interviewing the complainant and notarizing the complaint. Immediate supervisors of the employee are notified, who can assist (at the direction of IA) in the investigation. IA then interrogates the officer/employee who is given the *Garrity* warning, which informs the officer that s/he can be disciplined or fired for refusing to answer IA questions, although such information cannot be used to criminally prosecute them (Walker & Katz, 2008, p. 464). These interrogations are tape recorded, and employees can bring their own recorder as well. Employees can also bring a peer-member (of same rank) as long as s/he is not part of the investigation (no legal counsel is permitted). IA investigations include interviews with potential witnesses (i.e., civilians and officers), as well as reviewing possible audio/video tapes between complainant and employee. Completed investigations, by IA, are then forwarded to the district commander, who signs off and then forwards them to the division commander—the deputy chief. The final signature is reserved for the chief of police, who is in charge (with consultation from deputy chief) of all discipline if the investigation supports a sustained complaint. IA is charged with notifying the complainant and the employee of the final investigation findings (and possible sanctions). Disciplinary action can be appealed by the employee by submitting this request to the executive secretary of the hearing board within 10 days after the action is taken. Within 10 days, a hearing will take place to review the appeal, at which time the employee can bring counsel with him/her.

KPD discipline usually takes the form of documented oral reprimand, written reprimand, days off (without pay), demotion in rank/pay, or termination. Discipline is based on a progressive system where penalties are based on a classification system from Class A (most severe) to Class C (least severe). Penalties within class B and C are based on the number of officer offenses. For class A, the discipline is dismissal from the department.

KPD utilizes an early warning system designed to track potentially problematic police behavior—Professional Excellence Program. There are two types of reports that are generated as part of the department's Professional Excellence Program—a quarterly report and an annual report. IA oversees and maintains the program (and subsequent reports).

The triggering mechanisms for someone to be "flagged" as part of the quarterly Professional Excellence Program are four or more use of force reports, three or more vehicle pursuit reports, two or more complaints of misconduct, failure to take the mandatory annual physical, and five or more of any combination of selected criteria. The triggering mechanisms for someone to be flagged as part of the annual Professional Excellence Program are six or more use of force reports, six or more vehicle pursuit reports, four or more complaints of misconduct, failure to take the mandatory annual physical, and 10 or more of any combination of selected criteria.

Once an officer is flagged for a quarterly or annual report, IA submits their name to the chief of police. After the chief reviews this information, the officer's commander is notified. The unit commander is responsible for contacting the officer's immediate supervisor who completes the officer's Employee Analysis Report (including, for example, assignment, complaints and referrals, disciplinary action, vehicle accidents, on duty injuries, use of force reports, etc.). The report on the officer has to be completed and submitted to IA within 20 days. IA will generally convene a Professional Excellence Program Review Group within 10 working days. This group inspects the analysis report, determine whether or not an intervention is needed, and if an intervention is needed they recommend a plan of action. The primary elements that are part of the plan of action include: remedial training, referral to the Employee Assistance Program (EAP), transfer to another assignment, placement under structured supervision, and counseling or disciplinary action.

It is up to one's immediate supervisor to monitor the progress of those under a plan of action. This includes completing a monthly status report and submitting it to the district commander and the Professional Excellence Program administrator. After six months, the group will meet again to assess the progress of the individual. Recommendations by the group include: successful completion, extending the program beyond six months, referral for additional assistance, or other necessary action. It is up to the chief of police to approve these recommendations.

References

Goldstein, H. (1990). *Problem-oriented policing.* New York, NY: McGraw-Hill, Inc.

Langworthy, R. H. (1986). *The structure of police organizations.* New York, NY: Praeger Publishers.

Maguire, E. R. (2003). *Organizational structure in American police agencies.* Albany, NY: State University of New York (SUNY) Press.

McCluskey, J. D., Mastrofski, S. D., & Parks, R. B. (1999). To acquiesce or rebel: Predicting citizen compliance with police requests. *Police Quarterly, 2,* 389–416.

Sampson, R. J., Raudenbush, S. W., & Earls, F. (1997). Neighborhoods and violent crime: A multilevel study of collective efficacy. *Science, 277,* 918–924.

Walker, S. (2003). *Early intervention systems for law enforcement agencies: A planning and management guide.* Washington, DC: Department of Justice.

Walker, S., & Katz, C. M. (2008). *The police in America: An introduction (6th ed.).* Boston, MA: The McGraw-Hill Companies, Inc.

Chapter 4

Surveying Patrol Officers: Process, Success, and Lessons

Previous police culture inquiries have utilized surveys and interviews of officers in both the structured (e.g., Brown, 1988; Jermier, Slocum, Fry, & Gaines, 1991; Paoline, 2001, 2004; Terrill, Paoline, & Manning, 2003) and unstructured (e.g., Muir, 1977; Skolnick, 1966; Van Maanen, 1974; Westley, 1970) format. The current analysis of culture relies primarily on structured surveys of street-level patrol officers. In doing so, we use extant research to construct a variety of cultural survey items to assess the ways in which officers deal with the strains of the occupation. For the authors, this was a culmination of close to a decade of thinking about culture and suffering through other projects' incomplete measures. When given the opportunity to query officers about police culture, we developed a survey in a way that would afford us the most comprehensive picture of what various researchers were independently adding to the culture mix. Because this was not the only component of the survey, we had to efficiently construct our measures in a way to get the most *bang for our buck*. In the end, our Likert-type survey questions, that tapped all of the components of Paoline's (2003) monolithic model, afforded a unique opportunity to capture and analyze the primary dimensions of police culture.

The administration of the patrol officer survey, across seven police agencies (of which many had separate patrol stations) was an arduous task, even with a very detailed pre-site preparation plan. While it would have been more efficient and inexpensive to utilize an electronic mail survey from our home universities, we feared the response rate would have suffered. Instead, our research team chose to visit each of the sites, over an extended period of time, to administer the survey face to face. As we explain in this chapter, this can be a risky proposition; if this is not done carefully it can result in low response rates across entire shifts of personnel versus a non-respondent via email. In the end, we were successful in our efforts, although success (i.e., surveying all you set out to) varied across departments. Along the way, we documented a number of lessons for those interested in patrol officer surveys or the methodology in general (for other populations). In the chapter that follows, we detail the patrol officer survey in terms of the overall process, success, and lessons learned.

The Survey Process

Aim

We chose to survey a population of police officers assigned to street-level patrol functions, rather than selecting a sample of them, for a few reasons. First, since we were attending roll call sessions (i.e., pre-shift meetings where officers are informed of relevant daily information by an immediate supervisor, usually a sergeant) to survey groups of officers, across every shift, we decided to capture the population of all officers instead of a select sample. From a manpower perspective, we realized this would be worth the investment. From a practical standpoint, given the sensitive nature of the survey topics (i.e., police culture and the use of force), we did not want select officers to be suspicious as to why they might have been randomly chosen over others. In fact, our on-site protocol of project staff informing officers of the study, its aims, and confidentially assurances specifically noted that all patrol officers were going to be surveyed, and the target agencies were not being surveyed for something that they individually (or collectively) failed to do, or for something they did incorrectly.

Second, since the overall project also aimed to eventually link attitudinal survey responses to a variety of theoretically relevant behavioral outcomes (e.g., use of force, citizen complaints, lawsuits), we did not want to potentially risk missing, through a randomized process, some organizational members that may be of interest later, as our behavioral outcome data consisted of a population and not a sample. Finally, gathering a population of patrol officers would enhance the descriptive elements of our survey findings, minimizing sole reliance on statistical inferences when using samples. To accomplish our aim, we needed nearly as much preparation (and manpower hours) prior to going to our sites as we did to actually administer the surveys across all geographic locations and temporal shifts.

Pre-Visit Preparation

Prior to administering the survey to patrol officers, across each of the seven agencies, we utilized a protocol by which we could maximize our efforts while on site. Our team was going to be surveying for a week to ten days, with a plan to visit each roll call at least twice. Our pre-visit protocol started by identifying all departmental patrol officers, as well as when and where they were assigned. While this may seem relatively simple, at times, this was extremely complex. That is, we had to account for assignment changes by area and shift so when we arrived we would know who was where. This first step started by constructing a master roster of every sworn member of the agency. We then disaggregated those assigned to street-level patrol functions, and matched such personnel to daily patrol rosters. This provided us with a population of patrol officers to survey on our site visits.

The second part of the pre-visit protocol involved the survey "plan of action." That is, the most efficient way to maximize our site visit time whereby researchers could survey each shift, across the various precincts/districts, at least two times. The central component to this plan was adjusting to officers' scheduled days off. Project staff had to ensure that the days and times for which they planned to survey a particular shift would result in the expected officers being there. For example, if Squad B in District I of Department X had scheduled days off on Thursday, Friday, and Saturday, survey staff made sure to schedule times for this squad on Sunday through Wednesday. In smaller agencies, like Knoxville, this was rather simple to coordinate, while in departments like Charlotte-Mecklenburg this was much more difficult. Once the "plan of action" for a department was finalized, the research team was responsible for double checking a week prior to going on site to ensure that no assignment changes occurred. Since surveys would be hand delivered (by name) to individual officers during roll calls, project staff could deal with a single (or few) officer(s) who recently changed assignments, but administering and charting new surveys to an entire shift would be extremely problematic (if not fatal) in the field.

The final element to the pre-visit protocol was to prepare roll calls for our arrival. That is, we wanted to minimize the element of surprise and/or disruption of a shift's roll call by arriving unannounced. Our agency contacts, who provided us with direction for all data collection, were vital at this stage. Our contacts, usually a commander-level position from Internal Affairs (which was usually the repository for use of force and complaint data), were asked to either call, email, or send a hard copy memorandum to shift supervisors in charge of the designated roll calls to prepare them for our arrival. Agency contacts helped legitimize the survey, but were asked to only act as schedulers and not impose values regarding (or encouraging) officer participation. While we wanted all patrol officers to participate, by our own (as well as Michigan State's, University of Central Florida's, and National Institute of Justice's Institutional Review Boards) standards protecting the rights of human research subjects, we did not want to force/coerce participation.

Visiting the Agencies

Roll calls serve as a mechanism to discuss relevant organizational (e.g., change in policies and procedures, expectations, concerns, etc.) and community (e.g., *be on the lookout for*, crime trends, citizen conflicts, etc.) information as a collective whole. These meetings are approximately 15 minutes in duration, and are usually led by a sergeant/lieutenant. As depicted in the media portrayals of roll calls, they also usually end with a catch phrase for officers, such as "be safe out there." We targeted these meetings as a place to efficiently survey groups of patrol officers.

Our roll call visits started by providing officers with a brief overview of our project (which encompassed more than a survey of officers). As part of this discussion, researchers explained that this project was sponsored by the United States Department of Justice, and their agency was chosen because they represented a divergent use of force policy from the other research sites. As Chapter 3 illustrated, each of these agency's organizational and occupational environments differed. In addition, we also informed the officers that no individual or group of officers was being singled out for participation in this survey. We then informed the officers of the comprehensive scope of the project, in that we had been working with their agency for well over a year.

Following our project overview, we discussed important issues of informed consent, confidentiality, and anonymity. We started by explaining that officer participation in the survey was voluntary, and if they chose to participate, per federal and university IRB regulations, we needed their signed consent. This consent form was on the front of the survey and contained our (and our university's IRB) contact information should they have any questions or concerns. This was important because we did not want officers filling out the survey because they felt they had to.

While signed consent is important, it can also pose issues with research participants, especially those (like the police) that have historically been noted to be characterized by higher levels of suspicion (Rubinstein, 1973) and cynicism (Neiderhoffer, 1969). Our explanation of confidentiality addressed such a concern, as we assured the officers that their responses to the survey were *confidential* and *no one* (including their chain of command and the United States Department of Justice), outside of the project staff, would be viewing their individual surveys.

The final component of our introductory read off distinguished confidentiality from anonymity. That is, while the survey results were confidential, the respondents were not anonymous. Respondents would have been anonymous had we showed up and distributed surveys to groups of officers without tracking individually (e.g., Officer Tom Seaver). Because we wanted to eventually link attitudinal survey responses with behavioral data (e.g., use of force, arrests, complaints, lawsuits, etc.), and we also wanted to make sure that each officer from our pre-visit plan was accounted for in the survey process, we needed to identify survey respondents. In doing so, we created a unique identification number for each officer that was not connected to any official identifying officer number (e.g., badge number, payroll number, car number, etc.). Officers were instructed to alert project staff if this happened, and we would issue a new identification number. The randomly assigned identification numbers were printed on the last page of the survey, as well as on the consent form (which was stapled to the front of the survey). On the top right hand corner of the consent form was the officer's name, which we read off at each roll call in order to assure that each officer received a survey. This process would also allow us to document those who did not get a survey. Officer names were not on the completed survey, as consent forms were detached from the survey once it was handed to project staff. Project staff also separated and shuffled consent forms from the returned surveys. Officers were instructed to tear off the top right hand corner of their consent forms which had their printed name. Since we had the same identification number on both documents, we were able to match up completed surveys with corresponding consent forms.

The 116-item patrol officer survey, over one-third of which was devoted to police culture, took anywhere from 10 to 25 minutes to complete. We also administered an abridged version of the survey to roll call sergeants/lieutenants for the purposes of which we discuss below in our *lessons*. Project staff stayed the entire time to collect the surveys and to answer questions from officers regarding the survey. Officers were instructed to complete their surveys individually, and not to discuss any of the items amongst themselves.

Our survey dates and time spent on site differed across each of our police agencies. In Colorado Springs, we surveyed officers from September 10–17, 2007. In Knoxville, our survey team was on site on September 26, 2007, and from September 28–30, 2007. For Charlotte-Mecklenburg, researchers surveyed officers from October 18–31, 2007. In Portland, survey times were November 6–7, 2007 and November 10–11, 2007. The surveying process in Fort Wayne departed from the rest in that they did not utilize a roll call system. In this department, patrol officers simply reported to their assigned areas at the start of their shift. To adjust to this difference, we coordinated with the department's annual in-service training, where we administered the survey on November 5–10, 2007; November 12–14, 2007; and November 16, 2007. For the Albuquerque Police Department, project staff was on site from December 11–17, 2007 to administer the officer survey. Finally, Columbus officers were surveyed from June 15–23, 2008.

The amount of time and staff allocated for surveying varied across our agencies according to departmental size, spatial differentiation, and internal assistance. As much as we tried to ease the process by planning prior to going to each agency, the complexities of patrol operations made the survey process challenging at times. For example, the Knoxville Police Department, with only two patrol districts, organized joint roll calls across the East and West patrol districts enabling us to complete our survey in roughly four days. This type of assistance made surveying in this agency uncomplicated and efficient. On the other hand, Charlotte-Mecklenburg's patrol operations were dispersed among 13 separate divisions (with five to six shifts per division). This site required more surveying manpower than any other site, and the total time on site was roughly 14 days. In Portland, the five patrol districts covered large areas, and there were just three ten-hour shifts (all of which were the same time), which meant that researchers had to stay in one given district per day. Given the geographic and shift-related complications in these two agencies, we improvised our model and hired local graduate students, from the University of North Carolina at Charlotte and Portland State University, to assist in surveying officers. These students were trained, on site, and handpicked via recommendations from our academic research peers at these neighboring universities. This greatly assisted in efficiently administering the officer survey across a number of precincts/divisions and temporal shifts. Next, we discuss the success of or survey efforts.

Success

The success of our patrol officer survey was assessed in a few different ways including, but not limited to, the response rate of those we encountered at each roll call. What follows is a breakdown of our success in terms of how many (and what percentage of) patrol officers were at the roll calls we expected them to be present at, how many (and what percentage of) patrol officers we surveyed from the overall population, and how many (and what percentage of) patrol officers we surveyed from those who were physically present. The last assessment criteria is what most researchers usually utilize as the sole indicator of success (i.e., who did not decline to participate). Table 4.1 presents a detailed breakdown of each of these indicators of success cumulatively, as well as individually within departments.

Table 4.1 · Patrol Officer Survey Response Rates

	Columbus	Charlotte-Mecklenburg	Albuquerque	Portland	Colorado Springs	Fort Wayne	Knoxville	Total
Patrol Number	910	685	456	382	317	221	176	3147
Number at Roll Call	549	474	328	263	204	197	157	2172
Percentage at Roll Call	60.33	69.20	71.93	68.85	64.35	89.14	89.20	69.02
Number Surveyed	523	466	325	250	199	190	156	2109
Percentage of All Patrol Surveyed	57.47	68.03	71.27	65.45	62.78	85.97	88.64	67.02
Percentage of Patrol at Roll Call Surveyed	95.26	98.31	99.09	95.06	97.55	96.45	99.36	97.10

Recall that our aim was to survey all police officers with street-level patrol responsibilities, as those assignments (unlike administrative type ones) are most likely to deal with the strains of the street with citizens and within the organization with supervisors. As such, the majority of police culture studies have focused on such street-level personnel. The first row in Table 4.1 ("Patrol Number") presents the number of patrol officers that was expected, based on our *a priori* research plan, to be available for surveying. These numbers correspond to our agency descriptions located in Chapter 3. In all, we expected 3,147 patrol officers to be available at roll calls when project personnel arrived to conduct the survey.

The second row ("Number at Roll Call"), in Table 4.1, represents the number of patrol officers that were physically present to be surveyed during our roll call site visits. Even though we had a pre-visit plan in place to survey the population of patrol officers around their scheduled days off, what we could not control for were those who took an unscheduled day off, attended court, were injured, on military duty, suspended, or were not present due to some other circumstance. The percentage breakdown, across sites, of those present compared to those expected ("Percentage at Roll Call"), in the third (shaded) row, illustrates a pattern by departmental size, and to a lesser extent spatial differentiation, as there was a greater fit between row one and row two for the smaller, centralized agencies (i.e., Fort Wayne and Knoxville). In Columbus, we see the least amount of fit, presumably because bigger agencies that are dispersing patrol among multiple districts/divisions/precincts can possibly absorb the daily loss of patrol personnel in drawing from other areas to cover patrol beats, whereas smaller staffed agencies do not enjoy such flexibility. In all, 2,172 of the anticipated 3,147 officers (69.0 percent) were available to be surveyed by our research team.

The fourth row ("Number Surveyed"), in Table 4.1, represents a primary indicator of survey success. That is, the actual number of patrol officers that took part in the survey. In all, 2,109 patrol officers were successfully surveyed across the seven police departments. The fifth (shaded) row presents percentages of those surveyed in relation to the pre-visit expected number of officers ("Percentage of All Patrol Surveyed"). Again, we find variation across agencies (i.e., from 57.5 to 88.6 percent) patterned by department size and spatial differentiation. Collectively, we were successful in surveying just over two-thirds of those patrol officers who were officially scheduled to be present when our staff arrived on site.

The final (shaded) row, in Table 4.1, illustrates the percentage of patrol officers who were available at roll calls and participated in filling out our survey ("Percentage of Patrol at Roll Call Surveyed"). This is usually the sole indicator that researchers utilize when reporting "response rates" (i.e., those who did not decline participation). While there is minor variation across sites (ranging from 95.1 percent in Portland to 99.4 percent in Knoxville), the results illustrate that surveyors were extremely successful in getting officers to take the survey as long as they were physically present. *Cumulatively, our research team was successful in surveying just over 97 percent of the patrol officers at departmental roll calls (and in-service training in Fort Wayne).* Throughout this process, we learned several lessons about surveying police officers, which we share in the next section.

Lessons

Throughout the research process we learned several lessons about surveying police officers. We share some of the major ones for those interested in similar approaches as ours including, but not limited to, studies of police officers. Our primary aim, in sharing these experiences, is to ease the research process by providing assistance in minimizing potential mistakes or fatal flaws.

The Need for Proper Pre-Visit Preparation

One of the easiest things to underestimate is the difficulty in executing an officer survey, especially one that seeks to track respondents and non-respondents. Our pre-visit preparation involved the construction of spreadsheets of officers based on patrol rosters and daily assignment logs that parsed out where and when personnel would be working. Doing this for hundreds of officers is both time consuming and complicated. When on site there is enough to navigate (e.g., getting to each station across several shifts, perfecting your introductory read off, making last- minute adjustments) without having to map out your survey protocol. Arriving on site with your surveys ready to go will allow for a much smoother survey process, while also making yourself (and the project) look professional (see below). Even with an elaborate pre-visit protocol, we had to make adjustments to our rosters (i.e., for last minute assignment changes), which was especially challenging as moving one roster piece ultimately affected others.

Another major element of pre-visit preparation involved the survey itself. Pretesting the survey, preferably with the same occupational group that you are targeting, allows for an assessment of whether or not the questions and response categories are understandable. This process will also help approximate the amount of time the survey will take to complete. Obviously, utilizing questions from previous established surveys will assist in this process, while also contributing to the scientific method of research replication.

Pre-visit preparation, no matter how gifted the researcher, cannot be done alone. That is, agency assistance is paramount. In our case, we not only relied on our agency contacts (see below), but also sought the assistance of human resource personnel, patrol coordinators, and civilian secretarial staff in helping us devise our master patrol roster and map out assigned areas and shifts. In departments that frequently rotate patrol geographic and shift assignments, this is a much more arduous task and awareness of when these changes occur come from these internal contacts. In successfully implementing an officer survey, with similar aims as ours, one has to ensure that patrol officers are going to be where (and when) you think they will be when you are on site.

The Role of the Agency Contact

Without question, the most important person in allowing research access to a police department is the chief of police. Once access is granted, the importance of the chief, in terms of executing your research objectives, diminishes substantially, if not altogether. Over the course of two years at each agency, we can count on two hands how many interactions we had with the various chiefs. The single most important organizational member for the police researcher is the agency contact who is assigned to them by the chief of police. This person is your lifeline to the agency, the person who gets you to the people that you need to contact to gather your data. Regardless of your research question(s) and methodology employed, it is advantageous, especially in a paramilitary organization, to have an agency contact from an upper level rank (i.e., captain and higher). These organizational members usually elicit a degree of respect that will ease the process of acquiring information from a number of different departmental levels and units. They are also usually well-versed in the overall operations of the department (through, if anything, their length of service), and if they do not know where something is, they know someone who knows where that something is. To use a sports analogy, the agency contact is the point guard of a basketball team. Given our primary research questions, for which this project was funded (i.e., the use of force), our agency contacts were primarily upper level sworn personnel from Internal Affairs (IA) units.

For our officer survey, the IA agency contacts were vital in helping us coordinate and compile our master rosters, and (more importantly) preparing shift supervisors for our arrival in surveying their patrol officers. At the same time, researchers have to be aware of the context and history of police organizations (see below), as one's agency contact can also be problematic for certain organizational endeavors. In our case, we did not want our IA agency contacts taking us to (or appearing at) roll calls to conduct surveys of patrol officers. While the tension between IA and officers is not as tumultuous as it was 20-plus years ago, symbolically walking into a roll call room with a member of IA can still pose some obstacles, especially in light of assurances of survey confidentiality (see below). In one of our sites, a very well respected IA captain, serving as our agency contact, visited a precinct that he used to oversee while we were waiting for officers to arrive for roll call. The few officers that were present immediately joked "ut oh, what did we do wrong," as they walked over to shake his hand. In this case, it was not an issue for us in executing our survey, as he was very well received and there were only a few officers present, but it was certainly something to be cognizant of, especially for those who might not have been under his command while he was a division supervisor.

Getting the Shift Sergeant "On Board"

Preparing, and preparing others, for the survey is a big step in the research process, but the success in terms of getting officers to participate in your questionnaire hinges on the supervisor (usually a sergeant) who conducts the roll call. While the sergeant cannot ensure your overall success, he/she certainly can play a major role in your failure. Similar to what has been documented for organizational reform failures (e.g., team policing; Sherman, Milton, Kelly, & MacBride, 1973), middle manager disdain can influence subordinate behavior.

When a researcher walks into a roll call room, they should remember that they are in a sergeant's house and it is advantageous to tread lightly. For example, even though we had the endorsement of the chief of police and our upper level management contact, we could not just barge into a police precinct and tell a sergeant that we were going to survey his/her officers. At the same time though, we *did* have the backing of the organization and if we ran into outright resistance we could use that card. Using that card though, in a station house confrontation with a sergeant, could affect our pleas for "voluntary participation" of the lowest members of police hierarchy. Being respectful to a sergeant, and his/her shift-level immediate objectives, are key to garnering research support. In our case, we informed the sergeants of our project, and if they were not aware of our visit (most were), we briefly explained our aims and year-long working relationship that we had with their agency. We then noted that police business for officers should be handled first, and then we would follow with the administration of the survey. We also informed the sergeant that we would be asking him/her to participate in a shorter version of the survey that they could do with the troops (which helped legitimize the survey process for some patrol officers) or before/after roll call, should they have existing business that they would like to handle while the officers completed the survey. To our advantage, shift sergeants and patrol officers are accustomed to roll call visitations from others for organizational briefings (e.g., training personnel, legal advisors, intelligence units, etc.), so our presence was not totally foreign.

Presenting the Project to Patrol Officers

Standing up in front of 10–25 armed, uniformed police officers in their "house" can be an intimidating endeavor for any civilian. At the same time, your job as a researcher is to garner compliance from research subjects, which is directly a function of the way you present yourself and your research aims. This process starts with a project read off, which has to be concise, yet informative. The memorized project read off should be professionally presented with a degree of confidence, without coming across as arrogant. Unlike other research methodologies, such as systematic social observation, presenting yourself as a researcher of police (instead of a student of policing—see Reiss, 1971) is perhaps the best approach. Being available for clarification questions is also important, although speaking after the read off is best left to a minimum. Like regulating a college classroom following an examination, you do not want to create an environment where you are standing in front of a room full of individuals with chaotic banter.

It is also important to know your limitations. Yes, you have been endorsed to be at roll call by higher ups, and shift sergeants are allowing you roll call time to conduct the survey, but your success (e.g., response rates, analysis, publishing, etc.) depends heavily on officer participation. Just as one should be mindful of respecting a shift sergeant's house, police officers are at roll calls for a reason, and have a shift of patrol work ahead of them that they are responsible for. Some officers may want to hang around a station, but others despise the office and want to get out on the street. Efficiently moving them through the survey is important. For us, this was tricky given the 116-item survey that, at times, took close to 30 minutes to complete. During one of our visits, just as we handed out the survey to an entire room full of officers, a major call came in which required nearly all of the officers to immediately get on the street. The shift sergeant was in the process of explaining the urgency of this situation to our research staff, at which time we immediately collected the surveys and explained that it was "no problem" and we would return at another time. We lost an entire shift's worth of research effort, but our gesture went a long way with the group, as when we returned at a later day they unnecessarily apologized. Being respectful and minimizing minor mistakes at roll calls can spread quickly to other areas and shifts, and can directly affect the success of your survey endeavors.

Dealing with Non-Respondents

Unlike collecting other data from police agencies (e.g., use of force, complaints, arrests, calls for service, etc.), getting access to survey research subjects (in our case patrol officers) is just one step of the process. That is, when you are collecting official records the primary hurdle is getting the department to allow you to retrieve it. On the other hand, just because a department allows you to survey its members does not guarantee that you are leaving with any data. Dealing with research subjects, especially the non-respondents, in a group setting should be handled with care, as you want to minimize a snowball effect.

Coping with survey non-respondents starts with a couple of realizations. The first thing to realize, as a researcher, is that it is not personal. The individuals that are declining participation usually do not personally know you, and may have perfectly valid reasons for not partaking in the survey process. The second thing to understand is the choice to participate is probably already made up before you start handing out surveys, so any attempts to negotiate participation will probably be futile. The best approach is to accept the non-respondent, and to minimize the chances that others will decline participation from your incessant pleas to change someone's mind about the "benefits" of completing a survey.

Non-respondents come in two different forms: passive and active. Passive non-respondents simply choose to invoke their right not to participate, without affecting anyone else. In terms of a snowball effect, these individuals are of little concern. The active non-respondent, usually in a verbal manner, is the one who can affect group response rates. Handling these non-respondents is where training is crucial, as it is best to try and minimize their impact on others if a snowball effect is about (or beginning) to take place. In one of our roll call visitations, as we were passing out the surveys, a bellowing voice came from a side wall announcing "I ain't doing no survey." When the project staff looked up, an older uniformed patrol officer, who was holding a shotgun (one person on each patrol shift was responsible for carrying a shotgun) stated that "it was his last two days of patrol before retirement, and at this point he really didn't have to do anything." The researcher smiled at the officer and stated "I wouldn't either." The group laughed, and that was the only non-respondent on the shift. In that particular example, confronting the officer detailing the social science benefits of his survey participation would have had probably no impact on his decision and could have affected others. If the soon-to-be-retired gentleman would have started a charge among his peers to collectively decline participation, the research team would have been advised to intercede and engage in open group dialogue regarding the need to not miss an entire shift of patrol in the department. As we witnessed in a number of areas and shifts, individuals (not groups) were our non-respondents. Learning to accept the 63 officers (out of 2,172) that declined to fill out our questionnaire is simply part of the research process.

Deliver on Your Promises

In using this type of methodology, especially when traveling across different roll calls, be aware that what you do in one session (especially incorrectly) can follow you to the next. When the authors of this book were in charge of a large-scale systematic social observation, as graduate students, we reiterated this to our observers on a number of occasions. If you are assuring police officers that "what happens on the ride, stays on the ride" in that you will not be sharing ride information with other organizational members and observers, you have to be true to your word. In some instances, officers would ask observers who they rode with previously and whether it was a good ride (i.e., busy with exciting encounters). If the observers went on to detail that they rode with Officer Mike Schmidt on the morning shift in sector two and made three drug arrests, wrote 10 citations, and had three foot chases, how would the current officer believe the confidentiality assurances that the observer promised for the current ride? Central to this notion is understanding that your research participants are active, not passive. That is, if you are guaranteeing something to police officers, your actions have to support such promises, as simply stating something is not enough.

For our project, we paid close attention to how surveys were collected (and separated) at each of the roll call visitations. Because our read off promised respondent confidentiality, we did not want signed consent forms stored with (or near) the completed surveys. We utilized two different carrying cases to transport completed surveys and signed consent forms. We also periodically, in front of the officers, shuffled consent forms and surveys. We did this because we recognized the real fear by respondents that if some organizational members read their responses to sensitive subject areas like perceptions of departmental use of force policies, immediate and upper level supervisors, and citizens it could be uncomfortable for all parties. We also planned for a worst case scenario (i.e., we lost, or someone stole, our folders) whereby there would just be a stack of completed surveys with no names on them and a collection of signed (largely illegible) consent forms. Thankfully, this scenario never happened. If we were nonchalant about storing completed documents, or if we appeared to be overly friendly with roll call sergeants, we could be compromising our research integrity, which could have drastic consequences for our visits to other areas and shifts. As such, if you promise respondents something, even if it is small in magnitude, be sure to deliver on it.

Know the History of Your Department, Especially Problematic Conditions

Not being aware of relevant organizational history can be (at best) embarrassing or (at worst) fatal for your survey endeavors. Talking to your agency contact and public information officer(s) can be extremely beneficial in finding out the historical context, especially recent, for the department that you are researching. A few examples illustrate this point. In one of our sites, shortly before our arrival for data collection two patrol officers were fatally shot, both of which were on our departmental master roster. Had we arrived at roll call and read off these officers' names, it could have severely undermined our efforts. An innocent oversight like this, understandably, would not have been received well by any group, let alone police for whom burying a fellow officer reinforces cultural elements of solidarity and loyalty that those outside the occupational group are not supposed to understand (Lord, Crank, & Evans, 2004).

In another agency, we learned, while on site to conduct the survey, of extensive tension between organizational members of all ranks and the United States Department of Justice (DOJ). In recent history, the organization rejected DOJ's effort to impose a consent decree so much so that personnel were willing to, and did, contribute individual funds for legal fees. The National Institute of Justice (NIJ), under DOJ, funded our project and because police agencies are usually more familiar with DOJ (over NIJ) we referenced them as our funding sponsor in our roll call read offs. Had we done this in this department, we would have been met with a potentially fatal backlash by officers we were seeking assistance from. This bit of organizational history information was extremely valuable to our research project.

Sometimes departmental history can "do you in" even if you do not make a mistake. For example, although not part of this book, we did have an eighth site that was part of our project. The department's chief agreed to grant us full access to a number of sensitive official departmental records, like the other sites, but outright refused to allow us to survey his officers. After negotiating with the chief, in a closed door meeting where we explained the importance of the survey as one of our primary data sources (per our proposal and funding source), he agreed to the survey excluding all of the questions related to police culture. When we inquired as to why he was declining this section, but had no issue with his personnel being surveyed about the use of force, he documented a recent agency survey that was conducted by a consulting group that was brought in by city council. According to the chief, one city government agency was to be part of an organizational climate survey, and the police department was chosen to be the representative. The chief explained that he endorsed the survey, but was surprised (and thoroughly upset) when the group came back with the results whereby he was asked to "fix" and/or "respond" to the concerns of his officers. The chief said that he would not go through that again and would rather not know about the culture of his organization, even with our assurances that he would not be asked to respond to our survey findings. We did not press the issue with the chief because we had yet to complete the data collection at his department, and instead agreed to an abridged version of the survey that did not query patrol officers about culture.

References

Brown, M. K. (1988). *Working the street: Police discretion and the dilemmas of reform*. New York, NY: Russell Sage Foundation.

Jermier, J. M., Slocum, J. W. Jr., Fry, L. W., & Gaines, J. (1991). Organizational subcultures in a soft bureaucracy: Resistance behind the myth and facade of an official culture. *Organizational Science, 2*, 170–194.

Lord, S., Crank, J. P., & Evans, R. (2004). Good-bye in a sea of blue. In J. P. Crank *Understanding police culture*. Anderson Publishing.

Muir, W. K., Jr. (1977). *Police: Streetcorner politicians*. Chicago, IL: University of Chicago Press.

Niederhoffer, A. (1969). *Behind the shield: The police in urban society*. Garden City, NY: Anchor Books.

Paoline, E. A., III. (2001). *Rethinking police culture: Officers' occupational attitudes*. New York: LFB Publishing.

Paoline, E. A., III. (2003). Taking stock: Toward a richer understanding of police culture. *Journal of Criminal Justice, 31*, 199–214.

Paoline, E. A., III. (2004). Shedding light on police culture: An examination of officers' occupational attitudes. *Police Quarterly, 7*, 205–236.

Reiss, A. J. Jr. (1971). Systematic observation of natural social phenomena. In H. L. Costner (Ed.), *Sociological methodology* (pp. 3–33). San Francisco, CA: Jossey-Bass Inc.

Rubinstein, J. (1973). *City police*. New York, NY: Farrar, Straus, and Giroux.

Sherman, L. W., Milton, C. H., Kelly, T. V., & MacBride, T. F. (1973). *Team policing: Seven case studies*. Washington, DC: Police Foundation.

Skolnick, J. H. (1966). *Justice without trial: Law enforcement in democratic society*. New York, NY: John Wiley.

Terrill, W., Paoline, E. A., III, & Manning, P. K. (2003). Police culture and coercion. *Criminology, 41*, 1003–1034.

Van Maanen, J. (1974). Working the street: A developmental view of police behavior. In H. Jacob (Ed.), *The potential for reform of criminal justice* (pp. 83–130). Beverly Hills, CA: Sage.

Westley, W. A. (1970). *Violence and the police: A sociological study of law, custom, and morality*. Cambridge, MA: MIT Press.

Chapter 5

Adapting to the Strains of Policing: Evidence from Seven Departments

The disparate conceptualizations of police culture (outlined in Chapter 1) still predominantly revolve around the occupational version, whether it be in endorsing this monolithic perspective or using another one (i.e., organizational, rank, styles) to refute it. From an empirical standpoint, what is missing from all approaches is a full-scale examination of the various dimensions that constitute culture. Even among the occupational conceptualization, which if one picks up a policing textbook or journal article still represents the most popular view of police culture, comprehensive studies that capture all (or most) of the facets of the internal and external policing environments are non-existent. What often happens is that scholars' primary contribution is a synthesis of a variety of individual piecemeal studies and writings that concentrate on various features of culture. Paoline's (2003) monolithic model is one example, as is Crank's (2004) collection of police culture "themes."

Across other cultural perspectives, we find even fewer recent contributions. For example, empirical inquiries into purely organizational accounts of police culture (i.e., across various police departments) still largely rely on Wilson's (1968) work from the 1960s. In a similar vein, full-scale studies of the effects of rank on police culture have been non-existent since Reuss-Ianni (1983). The bulk of the most recent scientific knowledge on culture has utilized policing styles as the foundation for conducting quantitatively driven classification schemes of different "types" of policing adaptations to primary aspects of the work environments. This work, including our own, has relied on a subset (but

113

not all) of the attitudes commonly associated with police culture. Such deficiencies served as the primary impetus for our approach in this book.

In the present study, we aimed to construct measures (based on extant research, if available) that captured more than just part(s) of what culture covers. We also sought to do this across more than a single, or just a few, police department(s). Our prior work, based on Project on Policing Neighborhoods (POPN) data from two agencies during the community policing era, did not focus (or even have a dedicated section) specifically on police culture. For the current study, we were liberated by the fact that we could ask our own questions in the culture section of the agency survey (discussed in Chapter 4). At the same time, we were cognizant of our limitations in that we could not address all of the disparate cultural perspectives at once. In framing our approach, we decided to revisit the roots of police culture thought. That is, we developed questionnaire items that would tap patrol officers' orientations toward *each* of the constructs that were delineated in Paoline's (2003) monolithic model that synthesized the various independent contributions of the occupational perspective. Given that this was our initial introduction to the police culture area, and where the majority of researchers turn for some guidance in making sense of this often confusing area, this was the most logical place to revisit. As such, in cumulatively building science, we go beyond simply conceptually structuring a working police culture model; we also empirically examine it.

What follows in this chapter is an assessment of the ways in which patrol officers perceive their two primary work environments. In addition, we examine how officers cope with the noted stressful conditions created by their occupational and organizational environments. We also assess the extent to which the primary cultural outcomes of social isolation and loyalty are endorsed by officers. Finally, we examine the degree to which officers cumulatively embody all of the values of the occupational culture (i.e., perceptions of environments, coping mechanisms, and outcomes). We do this across seven police departments of varying size and structure. Recall, as outlined in Chapter 3, we categorized departments as large (Columbus and Charlotte-Mecklenburg), medium (Portland, Albuquerque, and Colorado Springs), and small (Fort Wayne and Knoxville). Overall, our survey data provide us with the methodological mechanism to examine the relative collectiveness (or heterogeneity) among officers, from several police agencies, as they deal with the various environmental strains of the occupation during a post-community policing era (see Chapter 2). For each of our survey items, we utilize Likert-type items with response categories that vary from "disagree strongly" to "agree strongly." For the analyses that follow, we code response categories so that higher values reflect orientations that are in *more* agreement with the cultural dimension under question. As such, some of our response categories had to be re-coded to accomplish such aims, and when this occurred we use italics to designate such changes.

The Policing Environments

Recall from Chapter 1 that police work within two primary environments, one that is external (i.e., occupational) and another that is internal (i.e., organizational). The occupational environment constitutes the interactions that police have on the streets with citizens, while the organizational environment comprises the exchanges that officers have with supervisory personnel in their given police department. Paoline's (2003) monolithic model of police culture identifies the defining elements of both of these environments. We begin with an examination of patrol officers' perceptions of these environments.

The Occupational (Street) Environment

Two fundamental elements comprise monolithic accounts of the police occupational environment—*danger* and *coercive authority*. Such traditional depictions of culture note the high degree of danger (i.e., actual and perceived) found out on the streets that officers patrol, and the unique coercive power that police wield (and must display) over citizens. The latter dimension often works to reinforce the former.

Danger

We asked officers to assess their degree of agreement regarding danger on the streets that they patrol, across three survey items that were adopted from Cullen, Lutz, Link, and Wolfe's (1989) dangerousness scale (see Table 5.1 on p. 133). One thing that is readily apparent is that, regardless of agency location, officers uniformly agreed that policing is dangerous. Interestingly, more officers agreed (and at higher levels) that their jobs were "dangerous" (question #1) and "a lot more dangerous than other jobs" (question #2), than when asked about their chances of "getting hurt" on the job (question #3). That is, over 99 percent of officers across all sites (regardless of size) were in agreement that they worked in a dangerous job, of which no less than 82 percent agreed "strongly." Comparing their occupation to other jobs resulted in very similar overall agreement levels, although we find more dispersion across agreements of "somewhat" and "strongly." In terms of actual harm (i.e., getting hurt), respondents from all departments, while still overwhelming agreeing with this survey item, were more split between responses of "agree somewhat" (from 37.3 percent in Portland to 47.6 percent in Fort Wayne) and "agree strongly" (from 41.8 percent in Fort Wayne to 52.5 percent in Portland) than the preceding two measures. When the items were combined to form an additive danger index, we find virtually identical means across departments, with a slightly higher value (11.0) among Knoxville officers. Interestingly, this was the smallest agency yet had the highest crime rate per 1,000 population (see Chapter 3).

Coercive Authority

Another aspect of patrol officers' work environment is the relative importance they place on displaying their coercive authority over citizens, which monolithic versions of police culture note can be a second source of occupational stress. We asked officers to respond to the following statement regarding this construct: "A good police officer takes charge of encounters with citizens" (see Table 5.2 on p. 135).

Similar to that of danger, we find consistently high levels of agreement (i.e., no less than 98.4 percent), across all departments, that officers need to display their coercive authority over citizens. With respect to the intensity of agreement, there is variation among agencies, with the most between the two smaller police departments. That is, just 71.1 percent of the officers from Fort Wayne "strongly" agreed with this statement, representing the least of all departments, compared to the highest in Knoxville at 84 percent. Despite this variation, there is relatively universal concordance among all officers regarding coercive authority, as we find that no more than 2.1 percent of respondents from any agency disagreed with this statement.

The Organizational (Supervisory) Environment

Monolithic versions of police culture identify *supervisory scrutiny* and *role ambiguity* as two defining facets of the organizational environment. Paoline (2003) explains that occupational conceptualizations of culture note the high degree of tension (and disdain) that patrol officers can hold toward supervisors who scrutinize their decision making *ex post facto*. In addition, officers are said to experience role ambiguity that is perpetuated by supervisory representatives of the police organization, who want their line personnel "on paper" to fulfill all policing roles (i.e., law enforcement, order maintenance, and service), yet only reward (and train) them for crime fighting functions.

Supervisors

Our first supervisor measure focuses on patrol officers' perceptions of their immediate supervisors. In doing so, we presented the following two survey items to officers, both of which have been used in prior research based on the POPN data (see for example, Paoline, 2001; Terrill, Paoline, & Manning, 2003): "My supervisor looks out for the personal welfare of his/her subordinates" and "My supervisor's approach tends to discourage me from giving extra effort."

Across both of these items (see Table 5.3 on p. 136), contrary to traditional characterizations of the monolithic police culture, officers from all departments do not uniformly display unfavorable attitudes toward their immediate supervisors. In fact, we find the opposite. That is, the large majority of officers, from each of the seven different police agencies, are positively oriented toward their immediate supervisors. That being said, we do find some variation in overall favorability. Across both measures, Knoxville held the most favorable assessments of direct supervisors (92.3 percent agreed that their supervisor looked out for the welfare of their subordinates and 88.5 percent disagreed that their supervisor's approached discourages extra effort). We find similar levels of positivity among our largest agency, Columbus (90.9 percent agreement and 81.8 percent disagreement, respectively). The least favorable views of direct supervisors, while still collectively positive, were found among our mid-sized Colorado Springs respondents, where 76.4 percent agreed that their supervisor looked out for the welfare of their subordinates and 73.8 percent disagreed that their supervisor's approach discourages extra effort.

Our second officer assessment of supervision focuses on more removed senior-level command personnel. We measured perceptions of top management based on agreement with the following three survey items, which like that noted above for direct supervisors has been utilized in a number of studies based on the POPN data: "When an officer does a particularly good job, top management will publicly recognize his or her performance"; When an officer contributes to a team effort rather than look good individually top management here will recognize it"; and "When an officer gets written up for minor violations of the rules, he or she will be treated fairly by top management."

As Table 5.4 (on p. 138) reveals, officers reported far less favorable views of top management than they did for their direct supervisors, yet not at the universal amount (and intensity) of disdain noted by occupational versions of police culture. In varying degrees, with the exception of Knoxville respondents, the majority of officers disagreed that top management would publicly recognize a good job (ranging from 92.1 percent in Fort Wayne to 67.4 percent in Colorado Springs and Albuquerque) and would recognize a team effort over an individual one (ranging from 84.1 percent in Fort Wayne to 57.6 percent in Albuquerque). Interestingly, we find the most positive views of top management with respect to treating officers fairly for minor violations of organizational rules, ranging from 22.6 percent agreement in Fort Wayne to 65.3 percent in Knoxville. This also illustrates the division among respondents regarding top management. An examination of the top management additive index reveals the least positive assessments among Fort Wayne officers (mean = 5.3), while Knoxville officers, as we see for several components of culture, expressed the most favorable views (mean = 7.7). Once again, we find the greatest contrast in officer perceptions between the two smallest police agencies.

Role Ambiguity

Another important cultural feature of the organizational environment of policing revolves around officers' perceptions of their role. In order to assess the extent to which officers believed their role was ambiguous, we presented them with the following three survey items (all of which were adopted from Rizzo, House, and Lirtzman, 1970): "There are clear, planned goals and objectives for my job"; "I know what is exactly expected of me"; and "I know what my responsibilities are."

Similar to views of direct supervisors (and to a lesser extent top management), our findings diverge from what traditional occupational characterizations of police culture would suggest. That is, across all agencies, officers expressed low levels of role ambiguity. As Table 5.5 (on p. 140) illustrates, well more than the majority of officers, in varying degrees, agreed that their job has "clear, planned goals and objectives" (ranging from 87.8 percent agreement in Knoxville to 66.9 percent in Portland). The same was found with regard to knowing "what is expected" of officers (ranging from 89.4 percent agreement in Albuquerque to 68.5 percent in Portland) and what their "responsibilities are" (ranging from 99.1 percent agreement in Albuquerque to 93.5 percent in Portland). Our findings also reveal that there was much more overall agreement, as well as "agree strongly" responses, in terms of officers knowing what their responsibilities are, compared to the other items. While perceptions of role ambiguity were low, the additive index illustrates variation across organizations. That is, Portland officers (mean of 6.1) expressed the highest degree of role ambiguity, while Albuquerque respondents (mean of 4.9) reported the lowest. As such, the greatest disparity between agencies in terms of role ambiguity exists among two of the mid-sized ones.

Coping Mechanisms/Cultural Prescriptions

The preceding section captured officers' views toward central features of their two work environments. The consideration of these environments is important because they both represent the arenas that shape police culture(s). In revisiting the definition, from Chapter 1, culture *comprises the attitudes, values, and norms that are transmitted and shared among groups of individuals in an effort to collectively cope with the common problems and conditions members face.* As such, we have covered the *common problems and conditions members face* aspects of culture, in detailing patrol officer perceptions of danger, coercive authority, supervisor scrutiny, and role ambiguity. The section that follows embodies the nucleus of police culture. That is, the various ways (and the degree to which) officers *collectively cope* with those factors that were identified in the previous section. Paoline's (2003) monolithic model delineated four principal coping mechanisms (or cultural prescriptions) that assist police officers in dealing with the strains of their occupation. Two coping mechanisms, *suspiciousness* of citizens and *maintaining the edge* over suspects during encounters, originate in the occupational environment on the streets, while two are formed through the interactions that police have with supervisors in their organizational environment—*laying low* and endorsing the *crime fighter orientation*. Patrol officers from our seven agencies were queried regarding their orientations toward each of these cultural prescriptions.

Dealing with the Streets

Suspiciousness

In evaluating the extent to which officers are suspicious (and distrustful) of citizens, as a way to cope with the danger found in the occupational environment, we relied on the following survey items, both of which were adopted from the POPN study: "Police officers have reason to be suspicious of most citizens" and "Police officers have reason to be distrustful of most citizens."

Across the two items, as illustrated in Table 5.6 (on p. 142), we find officers to be generally more suspicious than distrustful of citizens. There is also a good deal of variation within and across agencies, although such dissimilarity (like much of the previous attitudes) is not patterned much by agency size categorizations. In addition, the variation across respondents from all agencies is located primarily among the "disagree somewhat" and "agree somewhat" response categories. In terms of a majority of responses, Knoxville, Albuquerque, Charlotte-Mecklenburg, and Columbus respondents agreed that officers have reason to be suspicious of most citizens, while only Knoxville officers agreed that they have reason to be distrustful of most citizens. With respect to organizational disparity, Knoxville officers, who also were among the highest in their perception of danger, were far and away the most suspicious and distrustful (75 percent and 60.7 percent agreement, respectively), while Portland officers reported the least suspicion and distrust of citizens in their occupational environment (39.9 percent and 33.1 percent agreement, respectively).

Maintaining the Edge

A second occupational environment coping mechanism identified for dealing with the strains of properly displaying one's coercive authority is the need to "maintain the edge" over citizens during encounters. We constructed a single item to measure this attitude, where officers were asked their level of agreement with the statement: "When I first arrive on a scene or during any interaction with a citizen, I size up the situation in order to establish and maintain control."

Like that found for coercive authority (in the previous section), officers across all agencies nearly unanimously agreed in maintaining the edge over citizens (see Table 5.7 on p. 143), ranging from 97.2 percent in Albuquerque to 99.4 percent in Knoxville. The intensity of this agreement, while varying across the seven departments (but not patterned particularly by size and structure), was well over the majority, ranging from 65.7 percent of Portland officers agreeing "strongly" to 78.4 percent in Colorado Springs.

Dealing with the Police Department

Laying Low

The way that officers are said to cope with the organizational strains of unpredictable and punitive supervisory oversight is by adopting a lay low (and cover one's ass) attitude toward the job, where they realize that extra effort only increases the probability of bringing undue supervisory attention to themselves. We measured laying low with a survey item, adopted from Brown's (1988) selectivity dimension, as this was the way that he distinguished his two aggressive crime fighting officer styles. That is, the old-style crime-fighter, whose style most resembled the occupational perspective of police culture, was selective in that s/he prioritized serious crime situations over handling all types of violations (unlike the clean-beat crime-fighter). We present the following item to officers to measure laying low: "An officer is more effective when s/he patrols for serious felony violations rather than stopping people for minor traffic violations and misdemeanors."

Table 5.8 (on p. 144) indicates that officers, across all agencies, were not universally endorsing the cultural prescription to deal with supervisor scrutiny by laying low. That is, few officers agreed with the notion of prioritizing felonies over less serious events, ranging from 12.4 percent in Portland to 20.4 percent in Albuquerque. That being said, officers do not exhibit uniformly strong disdain for such an approach, as disagreement is concentrated among the "disagree somewhat" response category, ranging from 48.6 percent in Albuquerque to 63.5 percent in Fort Wayne.

Role Orientation

In dealing with the organizational strain of role ambiguity, officers who endorse the occupational perspective of culture are said to relieve such vagueness by endorsing the role that supervisors only officially recognize—crime fighting. As part of this coping mechanism, officers should also reject the functions that are not directly (and immediately) related to fighting crime (i.e., the maintenance of order and community policing). We examined officers' orientations toward each of these roles in Tables 5.9, 5.10, and 5.11.

Two survey items were utilized to measure officers' endorsement of the crime fighter role orientation: "Enforcing the law is by far a patrol officer's most important responsibility" (from the POPN study) and "Most patrol officers have to spend too much of their time handling unimportant, non-crime calls for service" (from Cochran & Bromley, 2003). While we find intra and inter agency variation (see Table 5.9 on p. 145), the majority of officers from all sites agreed in the crime fighter role orientation, although the level of intensity is concentrated among the "agree somewhat" response category. We also find that slightly more officers agreed that "enforcing the law is by far a patrol officer's most important responsibility" over "most patrol officers have to spend too much of their time handling unimportant, non-crime calls for service," although a higher percentage of officers across departments "agreed strongly" with the second item (i.e., 4) over the first (i.e., 3). Finally, whereas Wilson (1968) would posit that our larger agencies would be the most legalistic in nature, we do find that to be the case for one of them (i.e., Charlotte-Mecklenburg), although our smallest agency (i.e., Knoxville) was equally as legalistically oriented.

In querying officers regarding the order maintenance functions of the job, we utilized three survey items (see Table 5.10 on p. 147), all of which were adopted from the POPN study. We asked officers their relative agreement in terms of whether law enforcement officers should be required to do something about: "public nuisances (e.g., loud parties, barking dogs, etc.)"; "neighbor disputes"; and "family disputes."

Contrary to occupational accounts of police culture, officers are not over-whelmingly rejecting policing functions that do not include traditional crime fighting. The majority of respondents, from all agencies, agreed that they should be required to do something about public nuisances, ranging from 72.5 percent in Knoxville to 54.2 percent in Colorado Springs. Officers also believed that they should be required to do something about neighbor disputes, rang-ing from 77.1 percent agreement in Columbus (our largest agency) to 56.2 per-cent in our mid-sized Portland site. Finally, the strongest favorable order maintenance orientations were found for handling family disputes, ranging from 93.5 percent (49.1 percent agreed "strongly") in Albuquerque to 75.8 per-cent in Charlotte-Mecklenburg. In assessing the order maintenance additive index, the strongest overall orientations were found among Albuquerque and Fort Wayne officers (both with a mean of 9.0), while the least positive (of the positive) were found among Colorado Springs officers (mean = 8.2). As such, this suggests that the majority of officers appear to have rather expansive role orientations, as they cope by endorsing crime fighting functions, but not at the expense of also approving order maintenance functions. Such a finding is contrary to occupational versions of police culture.

The third role orientation that we captured was officers' perception of com-munity policing, or dealing with lower level disorder conditions. Like the pre-vious items, we asked officers their relative agreement with three types of problems, captured in the following three survey items (also from the POPN study): "Law enforcement officers should be required to do something about—litter and trash"; "Law enforcement officers should be required to do something about—parents that don't control their kids"; and "Law enforce-ment officers should be required to do something about—nuisance businesses that cause lots of problems for neighbors."

As Table 5.11 (on p. 149) reveals, officers' orientations toward community policing, across the board, were less favorable than that found for either law enforcement or order maintenance. We find that officers were gen-erally divided within and across agencies as to whether they should be required to do something about "litter and trash" and "parents that don't control their kids." The majority of Albuquerque (63.9 percent), Columbus (54.1 percent), Charlotte-Mecklenburg (50.5 percent), and Knoxville (50.3 percent) respon-dents agreed that they should handle "litter and trash," while the majority of Colorado Springs (63.8 percent), Portland (53.9 percent), and Fort Wayne (52.6 percent) officers disagreed. Even more disagreement was found for the requirement that police should have to handle situations where "parents don't control their kids," where majority agreement was only found among Colum-bus (59.8 percent) and Charlotte-Mecklenburg (50.6 percent) officers, while

Fort Wayne respondents were equally split between agreement and disagreement. By contrast, officers were far more accepting, from all agencies, of community policing functions that focused on "nuisance businesses," ranging from 74.7 percent agreement in Charlotte-Mecklenburg to 61 percent in Fort Wayne. That being said, the acceptance of such initiatives is not particularly intense, as agreement rests primarily within the "agree somewhat" response option, ranging from 56.2 percent in Knoxville to 47.5 percent in Albuquerque.

Cumulatively, in examining the additive index, we find the greatest acceptance for community policing among Columbus and Albuquerque officers (mean = 8.0), while the least is found among Colorado Springs respondents (mean = 7.1). Interestingly, we find that our three smallest agencies, including our smallest mid-sized one, are the least community policing oriented (i.e., most like occupational culture expectations). The fact that officers are generally less accepting of community policing initiatives (and only "somewhat" in their agreement), compared to tradition law enforcement and order maintenance functions, says something for the once popular policing philosophy.

Cultural Outcomes

The final component of Paoline's (2003) monolithic model identifies two cumulative outcomes. That is, the problematic conditions that officers are exposed to in their occupational and organizational environments, as well as the culturally prescribed coping mechanisms presented to deal with environmental strains, are said to contribute to two fundamental outcome-related features of police culture—a group that is socially isolated from the citizens that they serve and one that is extremely loyal to their fellow occupational peers.

The Occupational (Street) Environment

Social Isolation

The commonly cited social isolation outcome of the occupational environment is a result of officers having to deal with danger and coercive power on the streets, and their prescriptions of suspiciousness and maintaining the edge over citizens during their encounters with them (Paoline, 2003). We measured social isolation with the following three survey items: "Most people have no idea how difficult a police officer's job is" (Greene, 1989); "Given my choice, when off duty, I would rather hang around with non-police than other police officers;" and "In order to remain effective, the police officer should remain detached from the community" (Skogan & Hartnett, 1997).

As Table 5.12 (on p. 151) illustrates, respondents from all agencies were overwhelmingly in agreement that "most people have no idea how difficult" their job is, ranging from 98.1 percent in Knoxville (75 percent "strongly" agreed) to 93.4 percent (64.3 percent "strongly" agreed) in Colorado Springs. At the same time, officers have boundaries to their social isolation beliefs. When queried about their off-duty socialization, we find officers were much more divided in who they would rather hang around (i.e., non-police versus other officers). Whereas monolithic characterizations of police culture would posit that officers would prefer to hang around with other officers, only one department's officers supported such expectations. Knoxville respondents reported majority disagreement with this survey item (53.6 percent), the bulk of which was found in the "disagree somewhat" response category (43.8 percent). By contrast, the majority of officers from the rest of the departments agreed that they would rather socialize off duty with non-police over their professional peers, ranging from 69.5 percent in Portland to 60.4 percent in Colorado Springs. Interestingly, Reuss-Ianni (1983), in her study of rank cultures in the NYPD, noted similar findings (i.e., off-duty socialization patterns) as a reason for the bifurcation of the *street cop culture* into a second *management cop culture*.

Turning to our final measure, we find very few respondents, from any department, that believed that they should be "detached from the community" as a police officer "in order to remain effective." An examination of our additive index reveals modest levels of social isolation, where the most isolated were Knoxville officers (mean = 8.0), followed by respondents from our two largest police departments (mean = 7.7 for both). This is not too surprising given the traditional culture values exhibited by Knoxville throughout this chapter, and the relative size of Columbus and Charlotte-Mecklenburg, where the relational distance between the police and the public is usually greater than that found for medium and smaller police departments.

The Organizational (Supervisory) Environment

Loyalty

A second outcome, based in large part from organizational supervisory scrutiny and role ambiguity, as well as the prescriptions to lay-low/CYA in concentrating on crime fighting functions, is strong loyalty to other officers. Here, loyalty exists on more of an emotional level as officers seek the mutual support of their line-level peers in combating the stressors created by interactions with supervisors in their respective police departments. Loyalty is also about physical protection, as officers join forces to deal with the various strains in the dangerous and hostile occupational environment in their dealings with citizens.

Loyalty was measured with the following three survey items: "When I am on the street, protecting a fellow officer is one of my highest priorities"; "There is a camaraderie and bond among police officers that those outside of policing would not understand"; and "The code of silence is an essential part of the mutual trust necessary to good policing" (adopted from Weisburd et al., 2000).

Like that of social isolation, officers are loyal to their peers, but there are limits to such outlooks (see Table 5.13 on p. 153). In terms of the priority placed on protecting fellow officers on the street, the physical dimension of loyalty, we find unparalleled unanimous agreement (with intensity) across all agencies, ranging from 94.1 percent "agree strongly" responses in Knoxville (100 percent overall agreement) to 90.2 percent "agree strongly" in Portland (99.1 percent overall agreement). Beyond the physical facet of loyalty, the overwhelming majority of officers, in varying degrees of intensity, agreed in the emotional component as well (i.e., the camaraderie and bond). Agreement, while less than the first item, ranged from 94.8 percent in Knoxville to 85.7 percent in Portland. Our last measure demonstrates the limits of peer loyalty among contemporary police, as we find less overall agreement and more intra and inter variation by respondents. That is, the majority of officers from all agencies did *not* believe in the code of silence, which is based on the notion that officers should avoid "ratting" on fellow officers (and their policing transgressions) to supervisors, Internal Affairs Units, courts, the media, and citizens (Skolnick, 2002). In perhaps the single most cited (and foundational) study of police culture, Westley (1970) found that the "code of silence" was so strong that over 75 percent of officers he surveyed would perjure themselves in the court of law in protecting a fellow officer. An examination of our additive index, not too surprisingly, finds Knoxville to be the most loyal group (mean = 9.7).

In sum, in examining Paoline's (2003) monolithic model from beginning to end, some interesting findings emerge. For the supporters of occupational versions of police culture there is both good and bad news. The good news is that we find that officers from the seven departments support some of the universally shared attitudes that constitute police culture. More specifically, officers operating within contemporary police departments (of various size, structure, and location) collectively acknowledge the danger and coercive authority elements of the occupational environment, as well as the need for maintaining the edge as a coping mechanism. In addition, there is also widespread agreement among officers regarding the need to endorse the crime fighting role orientation as a mechanism to cope with the strains of the organizational environment. Finally, officers overwhelmingly believe in being loyal to their peers as long as it does not require the "code of silence."

The bad news for those who support occupational versions of police culture is that we also find varying degrees of divergence among this population of patrol officers. The analyses revealed that for some orientations the degree of collectiveness (i.e., well over the majority of officers) was opposite of expectations. For example, the shared orientations toward direct supervisors and order maintenance functions were generally positive, while officers were not experiencing role ambiguity nor believing in laying low. For other cultural components, we find heterogeneity in officer orientations (i.e., variation in agreement levels within and across departments), which contrasts the monolithic accounts of universal agreement purported by occupational perspectives. More specifically, we found divisions among officers in their suspicion (and distrust) of citizens, as well as their isolation from them. Moreover, in the organizational environment, we found variation in the disdain for top management and the rejection of community policing (non-crime control) initiatives.

While these findings inform us about the aggregate results, across each of these individual attributes, they do not tell us about the collective nature of cultural orientations. Put simply, responses indicate that patrol officers endorse some parts of culture more than other parts, but we do not know the degree to which officers (even if not the majority) endorse the full model. Paoline's (2001, 2004) research that developed a quantitatively driven classification scheme of police officers, found one style (i.e., 8.7 percent of the 585 officers) that embodied several of the values associated with the occupational police culture perspective. This work was based on results from two departments, as part of the POPN study during the community era of policing, and examined a subset of the cultural dimensions examined here. In the section that follows, we conduct analyses that allow for a more complete examination as to whether (and how may) officers embody the cumulative attitudes of the occupational perspective as culture carriers.

The Occupational Culture Carriers

We begin the examination of occupational culture carriers by creating a protocol to assess cumulative agreement across *all* of the dimensions described in the preceding analyses. Table 5.14 (on p. 155) displays the central features of this protocol. The first column (on the far left) lists each cultural dimension in order of overall agreement (i.e., from highest to lowest). The second column recalls the origin, on Paoline's (2003) occupational model, of each dimension (i.e., environment, coping mechanism, and outcome). Column three lists the total number of survey items that were utilized to measure each cultural dimension. The next column represents the overall criteria for establishing the threshold of cultural agreement for each individual dimension. In instances where a single questionnaire item was used, agreement was needed (either somewhat or strongly) to be counted. In instances where multiple survey items were utilized to tap a cultural dimension, which could have included different elements of that construct (e.g., the emotional and physical aspects of peer loyalty), we used a more relaxed criteria for assessing agreement. That is, in cases where two measures were employed, agreement (somewhat or strongly) with at least one was required, and when three items were used, agreement with at least two was the threshold.

The final column illustrates the agreement totals for each cultural construct across the 2109 patrol officers from the seven police departments. The total numbers (and percentages of the overall population) echo and summarize the aggregate findings from the previous section, although they incorporate a slightly more liberal threshold. Here, we see that 98.7 percent of the respondents agreed with the coercive authority component of the occupational environment, while (at the bottom) just over 10 percent agreed with at least two of the multi item measures of the organizational environment coping mechanism of role ambiguity. We use this ordering to "add in" each of the attitudes, by highest percentage of overall agreement (in our next analysis), to assess how the culmination of agreement progresses. Table 5.14 illustrates that cultural agreement, as one considers each item, progressively declines from widespread agreement (coercive authority, maintaining the edge, danger, crime fighter orientation, and loyalty), to majority agreement (top management scrutiny and citizen suspiciousness), to moderate agreement (social isolation and rejection of community policing initiatives), to some agreement (direct supervisor scrutiny and rejection of order maintenance initiatives), to slight agreement (laying low and role ambiguity). What this does not tell us is the collective agreement levels across multiple (or all) components of the occupational culture. For example, do the 92 percent of officers who believe in the crime fighting aspects of the occupational culture also support the danger, maintaining the edge, and coercive authority parts of the street environment? Likewise, do the 10 percent of respondents that view their role as ambiguous also endorse all of the cultural dimensions above it? The answers to such questions are presented in the next table.

Table 5.15 (on p. 156) presents the results of the analysis of culture carriers. Similar to Table 5.14, the column on the far left lists each of the 13 attitudinal constructs of the occupational perspective of police culture, ordered by the protocol established in the previous analysis. The difference here is that the consideration of each dimension incorporates the agreement levels among officers for that item as well as the dimension(s) above it. We begin with coercive authority because this construct received the greatest aggregate agreement totals (2082 or 98.7 percent of 2109 officers). When the next highest total item, maintaining the edge, is added, it represents all of the officers that subscribe to this cultural dimension and coercive authority listed above it (2053 or 97.3 percent of 2109 officers). This process is followed all the way through role ambiguity. Overall, this analysis allows for an examination of three things. First, it sheds light on the cumulative nature of cultural agreement, as we gradually consider the collection of all the attitudinal dimensions. This is accomplished at the aggregate (i.e., combining all officers), as well as across each of the seven individual police departments. Second, it illustrates important cutoff points of agreement across the various attitudinal dimensions. That is, how much of Paoline's (2003) model is cumulatively supported by segments of officers, when it is strongest, and where does it break down? Finally, it tells us the extent to which officers were true culture carriers (i.e., embodied all of the values of the occupational perspective).

In examining the cumulative nature of the cultural dimensions, we find very tight clustering among the first three orientations. That is, roughly 95 percent of all officers agreed with the coercive authority, maintaining the edge, and danger components of occupational culture, with very slight variation across agencies. Once crime fighting and loyalty are added to the mix, we still find high levels of aggregate commitment across officers, with only subtle progressive reductions in culture carriers (i.e., 6.3 percent when adding crime fighting and then 7.2 percent when loyalty was considered). We also find that 89.1 percent of Knoxville officers cumulatively align with these five cultural dimensions, compared to 71.6 percent of those working for the Portland Police Bureau. *Overall, these five aspects of culture (i.e., coercive authority, maintaining the edge, danger, crime fighter orientation, and loyalty) represent the most powerful elements of occupational collectiveness among police.* Interestingly, these features of occupational culture also coincide with many of the "machismo" (Herbert, 1998) characterizations of police officers as a crime fighting, loyal group that have to deal with danger and utilizing coercive power on the streets by being one up on citizens at all times (Drummond, 1976; Van Maanen, 1974).

The addition of disdain for unsupportive top management represents one of the critical drop-off points in assessing cultural carriers. At the aggregate, we still find endorsement by the majority (53.3 percent) of patrol officers, although we do not find majority agreement among three of the seven agencies (i.e., Knoxville, Albuquerque, and Portland). This is also where a significant amount of Knoxville officers, who were leading the pack of culture carriers, drop out. Over 50 percent of Knoxville respondents are removed (from 89.1 to 38.5) once negative views of top management are expected of officers. Put simply, there is a cultural game changer for Knoxville officers, who express (contrary to the occupational perspective) the most favorable views of top management over all over departments (recall Table 5.4). The least drop off is found in Fort Wayne at 10.5 percent. At no point for the rest of the way do we find the existence of a majority of culture carriers, either at the aggregate or for any individual department.

Next, we turn to the incorporation of two features of the occupational street environment, suspiciousness and social isolation from citizens. Roughly one-third and 17.6 percent of all officers are still regarded as culture carriers, with the highest percentage among the Fort Wayne Police Department (44.2 and 22.6 percent, respectively) and the fewest among the Portland Police Bureau (22.4 and 10.4 percent, respectively). So, when we considered agreement levels of suspicion and social isolation individually (in Table 5.14) we found that the majority (58.5 percent for suspiciousness) or near majority (45.6 percent for social isolation) endorsed these cultural outlooks, but when we examine the cumulative impact there are significantly fewer culture carriers.

When we add rejecting roles other than crime fighting (i.e., community policing initiatives), just 8.8 percent of the population are culture carriers, with agency-level variation from 13.7 percent in Fort Wayne to 5.6 percent in Portland. The incorporation of the final four organizationally driven cultural features results in substantial drop offs in culture carriers from just a few (i.e., 3.1 percent when adding disdain for direct supervisors and 1.6 when adding rejecting order maintenance functions) to nearly none (i.e., 0.4 percent when adding laying low from supervisors and 0.1 when adding role ambiguity). After cumulatively considering 13 dimensions of the occupational police culture (i.e., environments, coping mechanisms, and outcomes), we find just two of 2109 officers (one from Charlotte-Mecklenburg and one from Portland) that would be regarded as true culture carriers. The implications of these findings are considered in the next chapter.

A Note on Socialization

One of the common errors that students of policing make is that they equate *socialization* with *culture*, using these two terms interchangeably. While they are certainly related, they represent distinct and separate concepts. Throughout this book we have focused on defining, outlining, detailing, and analyzing police culture. The way(s) in which culture(s) is/are transmitted across occupational members is through the socialization process. As Klofas, Stojkovic, and Kalinich (1989, p. 150) explain, "occupational socialization is the process by which a person acquires the values, attitudes, and behaviors of an ongoing occupational social system." In the simplest sense, for distinction, *socialization* involves teaching and learning, while the substance of what is taught and what you learn is *culture*. Brown (1988, p. 243) details how socialization operates among police officers: "patrolmen undergo an intense rite of passage in which they acquire some general precepts of police work and learn the norms that govern police culture."

In policing, like that of many occupations, socialization experiences are heightened during the early stages of one's career. At the same time, socialization represents an ongoing process that evolves over time (McNamara, 1999). The learning process also contains formal and informal elements. In policing, the formal elements comprise one's academy (and in-service) training, policies, standard operating procedures/directives, and so forth, while the informal elements come from one's fellow officers, field training and senior-level officers, supervisors, citizens, etc. The formal aspects of socialization usually focus on the "here's what to expect and how to properly handle" various facets of police work, while the informal aspects tend to focus on the "here's how the real world operates." To date, the most eloquent study of police socialization was conducted, through participant observation (longitudinally, over a two-and-a-half-year period) by John Van Maanen (1974). Van Maanen described four distinct stages of socialization that actually starts before one is officially hired as a police officer, as officers go through various selection phases before they are chosen to attend the police academy (i.e., "choice"). The remaining three stages that Van Maanen identified carry through several critical points of an officer's development, and include: "introduction" (i.e., the police training academy), "encounter" (i.e., the initial teachings of one's field training officer and patrol peers), and "metamorphosis" (i.e., when one discovers the true realities of the occupation).

Given the importance of socialization in understanding culture, we assessed the relative strength of socialization across agencies. In doing so, we constructed the following three survey items, each of which (like several of the previous cultural elements) tap different dimensions of teaching and learning: "When I started my policing career, other officers were a valuable source of information on how to perform as an officer"; "Most of what I know about policing was learned 'on the job'"; and "I try to teach younger officers how to perform their duties as an officer."

We begin with a consideration of officers' assessments regarding the influence of early socialization experiences when they started their policing careers. As Table 5.16 (on p. 158) illustrates, officers from all departments overwhelmingly agreed that such processes were valuable in learning the skills of the job, ranging from 100 percent in Knoxville to 97.8 percent in Albuquerque. The intensity of agreement was also present for this dimension of socialization, as no less than two-thirds of officers from any of the seven departments agreed "strongly" with this questionnaire item. Our second dimension of socialization measures learning that has occurred over the course of an officer's career beyond their initial introduction to the occupation. Once again, we find the majority of officers uniformly agreed that most of their policing knowledge was learned "on the job," although the percentage of overall agreement (and intensity) across departments is less than that found for the first item. Our last socialization measure switches the attention to the officer as a teacher versus that of a student. Officers, from all departments, appear to be willing to pass the torch of policing knowledge on to their younger peers, as there is widespread agreement reported (ranging from 96.1 percent in Knoxville to 92.4 percent in Charlotte-Mecklenburg). The additive index reveals very similar scores, albeit slightly higher in the larger and mid-size agencies, regarding the importance of socialization (i.e., teaching and learning) among officers. Cumulatively, such orientations are consistent with what Van Maanen (1974) concluded nearly 40 years ago.

References

Brown, M. K. (1988). *Working the street: Police discretion and the dilemmas of reform*. New York, NY: Russell Sage Foundation.

Cochran, J. K., & Bromley, M. L. (2003). The myth(?) of the police sub-culture. *Policing: An International Journal of Police Strategies & Management, 26*, 88–117.

Crank, J. P. (2004). *Understanding police culture* 2nd ed. Cincinnati, OH: Anderson Publishing.

Cullen, F. T., Lutze, F. E., Link, B. G., & Wolfe, N. T. (1989). The correctional orientation of prison guards: Do officers support rehabilitation? *Federal Probation, 53*, 34–41.

Drummond, D. S. (1976). *Police culture*. Beverly Hills, CA: Sage.

Greene, J. R. (1989). Police officer job satisfaction and community perceptions: Implications for community policing. *Journal of Research in Crime and Delinquency, 26*, 168–183.

Herbert, S. (1998). Police subculture reconsidered. *Criminology, 36*, 343–370.

Klofas, J., Stojkovic, S., & Kalinich, D. (1989). *Criminal justice organizations: Administration and management.* Pacific Grove, CA: Brooks/Cole Publishing Co.

McNamara, R. P. (1999). The socialization of the police. *Police and policing: Contemporary issues, 2*, 1–12.

Paoline, E. A., III. (2001). *Rethinking police culture: Officers' occupational attitudes.* New York, NY: LFB Publishing.

Paoline, E. A., III. (2003). Taking stock: Toward a richer understanding of police culture.*Journal of Criminal Justice, 31*, 199–214.

Paoline, E. A., III. (2004). Shedding light on police culture: An examination of officers' occupational attitudes. *Police Quarterly, 7*, 205–236.

Reuss-Ianni, E. (1983). *Two cultures of policing.* New Brunswick, NJ: Transaction.

Rizzo, J. R., House, R. J., & Lirtzman, S. I. (1970). Role conflict and ambiguity in complex organizations. *Administrative Science Quarterly, 15*, 150–163.

Skogan, W. G., & Hartnett, S. M. (1997). *Community policing, Chicago style.* New York, NY: Oxford University Press.

Skolnick, J. H. (2002). Corruption and the blue code of silence. *Police Practice and Research, 3*, 7–19.

Terrill, W., Paoline, E. A., III, & Manning, P. K. (2003). Police culture and coercion. *Criminology, 41*, 1003–1034.

Van Maanen, J. (1974). Working the street: A developmental view of police behavior. In H. Jacob (Ed.), *The potential for reform of criminal justice* (pp. 83–128). Beverly Hills, CA: Sage.

Weisburd, D., Greenspan, R., Hamilton, E. E., Williams, H., & Bryant, K. A. (2000). *Police attitudes toward abuse of authority: Findings from a national study.* Washington, DC: National Institute of Justice Research in Brief.

Westley, W. A. (1970). *Violence and the police: A sociological study of law, custom, and morality.* Cambridge, MA: MIT Press.

Wilson, J. Q. (1968). *Varieties of police behavior: The management of law and order in eight communities.* Cambridge, MA: Harvard University Press.

Table 5.1 · Perceptions of the Occupational Environment: Danger

Survey Items	Columbus	Charlotte-Mecklenburg	Portland	Albuquerque	Colorado Springs	Fort Wayne	Knoxville
I Work In A Dangerous Job							
Disagree Strongly	0 (0.0)	1 (0.2)	0 (0.0)	0 (0.0)	1 (0.5)	0 (0.0)	0 (0.0)
Disagree Somewhat	4 (0.8)	1 (0.2)	1 (0.4)	1 (0.3)	0 (0.0)	1 (0.5)	0 (0.0)
Agree Somewhat	86 (16.5)	69 (14.8)	35 (14.1)	51 (15.8)	25 (12.6)	24 (12.6)	21 (13.5)
Agree Strongly	430 (82.7)	395 (84.8)	212 (85.5)	271 (83.9)	173 (86.9)	165 (85.8)	135 (86.5)
My Job Is A Lot More Dangerous Than Other Kinds Of Jobs							
Disagree Strongly	1 (0.2)	2 (0.4)	1 (0.4)	1 (0.3)	1 (0.5)	1 (0.5)	0 (0.0)
Disagree Somewhat	24 (4.6)	18 (3.9)	12 (4.9)	13 (4.0)	7 (3.5)	12 (6.3)	3 (2.0)
Agree Somewhat	192 (37.1)	131 (28.2)	87 (35.7)	81 (25.1)	63 (31.8)	72 (37.9)	51 (33.3)
Agree Strongly	301 (58.1)	313 (67.5)	144 (59.0)	228 (70.6)	127 (64.1)	105 (55.3)	99 (64.7)

Table 5.1 · Perceptions of the Occupational Environment: Danger, *cont.*

Survey Items	Columbus	Charlotte-Mecklenburg	Portland	Albuquerque	Colorado Springs	Fort Wayne	Knoxville
In My Job, A Person Stands A Good Chance Of Getting Hurt							
Disagree Strongly	5 (1.0)	4 (0.9)	3 (1.2)	7 (2.2)	2 (1.0)	3 (1.6)	1 (0.7)
Disagree Somewhat	41 (7.9)	35 (7.5)	22 (9.0)	33 (10.2)	12 (6.0)	17 (9.0)	5 (3.3)
Agree Somewhat	215 (41.5)	190 (40.9)	91 (37.3)	138 (42.6)	92 (46.2)	90 (47.6)	68 (44.4)
Agree Strongly	257 (49.6)	235 (50.6)	128 (52.5)	146 (45.1)	93 (46.7)	79 (41.8)	79 (51.6)
Additive Index							
Mean	10.8	10.9	10.8	10.8	10.8	10.6	11.0
Median	11.0	11.0	11.0	11.0	11.0	11.0	11.0
Range	6-12	5-12	6-12	6-12	7-12	5-12	7-12
N	515	463	242	321	198	189	153

Table 5.2 · Perceptions of the Occupational Environment: Coercive Authority

Survey Items	Columbus	Charlotte-Mecklenburg	Portland	Albuquerque	Colorado Springs	Fort Wayne	Knoxville
A Good Police Officer Takes Charge Of Encounters With Citizens							
Disagree Strongly	0 (0)	0 (0)	1 (0.4)	0 (0)	1 (0.5)	0 (0)	0 (0)
Disagree Somewhat	4 (0.8)	4 (0.9)	3 (1.2)	1 (0.3)	1 (0.5)	4 (2.1)	1 (0.6)
Agree Somewhat	113 (21.7)	85 (18.2)	61 (24.6)	60 (18.6)	40 (20.1)	51 (26.8)	24 (15.4)
Agree Strongly	403 (77.5)	377 (80.9)	183 (73.8)	262 (81.1)	157 (78.9)	135 (71.1)	131 (84.0)
Mean	3.8	3.8	3.7	3.8	3.8	3.7	3.8
Median	4.0	4.0	4.0	4.0	4.0	4.0	4.0
N	520	466	248	323	199	190	156

Table 5.3 · Perceptions of the Organizational Environment: Direct Supervisors

Survey Items	Columbus	Charlotte-Mecklenburg	Portland	Albuquerque	Colorado Springs	Fort Wayne	Knoxville
My Supervisor Looks Out For The Welfare Of His/Her Subordinates							
Disagree Strongly	9 (1.7)	25 (5.4)	10 (4.0)	8 (2.5)	12 (6.0)	15 (7.9)	5 (3.2)
Disagree Somewhat	38 (7.4)	54 (11.7)	34 (13.8)	24 (7.5)	35 (17.6)	26 (13.7)	7 (4.5)
Agree Somewhat	204 (39.6)	204 (44.4)	128 (51.8)	122 (37.9)	88 (44.2)	94 (49.5)	66 (42.6)
Agree Strongly	264 (51.3)	178 (38.5)	75 (30.4)	168 (52.2)	64 (32.2)	55 (28.9)	77 (49.7)
My Supervisor's Approach Tends to Discourage Me from Giving Extra Effort							
Agree Strongly	18 (3.5)	25 (5.4)	14 (5.7)	17 (5.3)	14 (7.1)	12 (6.3)	5 (3.2)
Agree Somewhat	76 (14.7)	84 (18.1)	34 (13.9)	46 (14.3)	38 (19.2)	29 (15.3)	13 (8.3)
Disagree Somewhat	169 (32.8)	180 (38.7)	105 (42.9)	109 (33.9)	91 (46.0)	75 (39.5)	63 (40.4)
Disagree Strongly	253 (49.0)	176 (37.8)	92 (37.6)	150 (46.6)	55 (27.8)	74 (38.9)	75 (48.1)

Table 5.3 · Perceptions of the Organizational Environment: Direct Supervisors, *cont.*

Survey Items	Columbus	Charlotte-Mecklenburg	Portland	Albuquerque	Colorado Springs	Fort Wayne	Knoxville
Additive Index							
Mean	6.7	6.3	6.2	6.6	6.0	6.1	6.7
Median	7.0	6.0	6.0	7.0	6.0	6.0	7.0
Range	2-8	2-8	2-8	2-8	2-8	2-8	2-8
N	513	462	245	322	198	190	155

Table 5.4 · Perceptions of the Organizational Environment: Top Management

Survey Items	Columbus	Charlotte-Mecklenburg	Portland	Albuquerque	Colorado Springs	Fort Wayne	Knoxville
When An Officer Does a Particularly Good Job, Top Management (TM) Will Publicly Recognize His/Her Performance							
Disagree Strongly	186 (36.0)	165 (35.6)	105 (43.0)	97 (30.4)	64 (32.2)	98 (51.9)	19 (12.4)
Disagree Somewhat	233 (45.1)	167 (36.0)	86 (35.2)	118 (37.0)	70 (35.2)	76 (40.2)	58 (37.9)
Agree Somewhat	87 (16.8)	113 (24.4)	48 (19.7)	90 (28.2)	60 (30.2)	12 (6.3)	64 (41.8)
Agree Strongly	11 (2.1)	19 (4.1)	5 (2.0)	14 (4.4)	5 (2.5)	3 (1.6)	12 (7.8)
When An Officer Contributes To A Team Effort Rather Than Look Good Individually, TM Will Recognize It							
Disagree Strongly	143 (27.9)	106 (23.0)	65 (26.7)	69 (21.5)	56 (28.4)	69 (36.5)	10 (6.5)
Disagree Somewhat	247 (48.2)	166 (36.0)	100 (41.2)	116 (36.1)	79 (40.1)	90 (47.6)	59 (38.6)
Agree Somewhat	111 (21.7)	162 (35.1)	71 (29.2)	118 (36.8)	53 (26.9)	25 (13.2)	71 (46.4)
Agree Strongly	11 (2.1)	27 (5.9)	7 (2.9)	18 (5.6)	9 (4.6)	5 (2.6)	13 (8.5)

Table 5.4 · Perceptions of the Organizational Environment: Top Management, *cont.*

Survey Items	Columbus	Charlotte-Mecklenburg	Portland	Albuquerque	Colorado Springs	Fort Wayne	Knoxville
When An Officer Gets Written Up For Minor Violations Of The Rules, He/She Will Be Treated Fairly By TM							
Disagree Strongly	68 (13.3)	57 (12.3)	51 (20.9)	46 (14.4)	36 (18.1)	55 (28.9)	14 (9.2)
Disagree Somewhat	204 (39.9)	172 (37.1)	91 (37.3)	112 (35.1)	74 (37.2)	92 (48.4)	39 (25.5)
Agree Somewhat	212 (41.5)	198 (42.8)	90 (36.9)	138 (43.3)	80 (40.2)	39 (20.5)	83 (54.2)
Agree Strongly	27 (5.3)	36 (7.8)	12 (4.9)	23 (7.2)	9 (4.5)	4 (2.1)	17 (11.1)
Additive Index							
Mean	6.2	6.7	6.1	6.8	6.4	5.3	7.7
Median	6.0	7.0	6.0	7.0	6.0	6.0	8.0
Range	3-12	3-12	3-12	3-12	3-12	3-12	3-12
N	507	461	241	314	197	189	153

Table 5.5 · Perceptions of the Organizational Environment: Role Ambiguity

Survey Items	Columbus	Charlotte-Mecklenburg	Portland	Albuquerque	Colorado Springs	Fort Wayne	Knoxville
There Are Clear, Planned Goals And Objectives For My Job							
Agree Strongly	146 (28.1)	129 (27.7)	41 (16.7)	118 (36.5)	46 (23.1)	31 (16.4)	53 (34.0)
Agree Somewhat	275 (52.9)	225 (48.3)	123 (50.2)	156 (48.3)	99 (49.7)	113 (59.8)	84 (53.8)
Disagree Somewhat	81 (15.6)	87 (18.7)	59 (24.1)	40 (12.4)	44 (22.1)	35 (18.5)	15 (9.6)
Disagree Strongly	18 (3.5)	25 (5.4)	22 (9.0)	9 (2.8)	10 (5.0)	10 (5.3)	4 (2.6)
I Know What Is Exactly Expected Of Me							
Agree Strongly	180 (34.7)	169 (36.6)	41 (16.7)	127 (39.4)	63 (31.7)	37 (19.5)	54 (35.5)
Agree Somewhat	282 (54.4)	225 (48.7)	127 (51.8)	161 (50.0)	98 (49.2)	110 (57.9)	76 (50.0)
Disagree Somewhat	53 (10.2)	59 (12.8)	65 (26.5)	33 (10.2)	33 (16.6)	35 (18.4)	19 (12.5)
Disagree Strongly	3 (0.6)	9 (1.9)	12 (4.9)	1 (0.3)	5 (2.5)	8 (4.2)	3 (2.0)

Table 5.5 · Perceptions of the Organizational Environment: Role Ambiguity, *cont.*

Survey Items	Columbus	Charlotte-Mecklenburg	Portland	Albuquerque	Colorado Springs	Fort Wayne	Knoxville
I Know What My Responsibilities Are							
Agree Strongly	290 (56.1)	261 (56.4)	116 (47.2)	192 (59.3)	103 (51.8)	87 (45.8)	92 (60.1)
Agree Somewhat	219 (42.4)	182 (39.3)	114 (46.3)	129 (39.8)	84 (42.2)	89 (46.8)	55 (35.9)
Disagree Somewhat	8 (1.5)	16 (3.5)	14 (5.7)	3 (0.9)	10 (5.0)	11 (5.8)	5 (3.3)
Disagree Strongly	0 (0)	4 (0.9)	2 (0.8)	0 (0)	2 (1.0)	3 (1.6)	1 (0.7)
Additive Index							
Mean	5.2	5.3	6.1	4.9	5.5	5.8	5.1
Median	5.0	5.0	6.0	5.0	6.0	6.0	5.0
Range	3-10	3-12	3-12	3-9	3-12	3-12	3-12
N	516	462	242	320	199	189	152

Table 5.6 · Adherence to Cultural Prescriptions: Suspiciousness

Survey Items	Columbus	Charlotte-Mecklenburg	Portland	Albuquerque	Colorado Springs	Fort Wayne	Knoxville
Police Officers Have Reason To Be Suspicious of Most Citizens							
Disagree Strongly	47 (9.1)	33 (7.1)	28 (11.4)	26 (8.1)	29 (14.6)	18 (9.5)	7 (4.5)
Disagree Somewhat	207 (40.0)	166 (35.9)	120 (48.8)	112 (34.9)	71 (35.9)	79 (41.6)	32 (20.5)
Agree Somewhat	221 (42.7)	194 (41.9)	86 (35.0)	133 (41.4)	75 (37.9)	84 (44.2)	80 (51.3)
Agree Strongly	42 (8.1)	70 (15.1)	12 (4.9)	50 (15.6)	23 (11.6)	9 (4.7)	37 (23.7)
Police Officers Have Reason To Be Distrustful of Most Citizens							
Disagree Strongly	69 (13.4)	58 (12.6)	50 (20.4)	37 (11.4)	34 (17.2)	23 (12.2)	11 (7.2)
Disagree Somewhat	214 (41.6)	188 (40.7)	114 (46.5)	136 (42.0)	78 (39.4)	81 (42.9)	49 (32.0)
Agree Somewhat	206 (40.0)	174 (37.7)	72 (29.4)	118 (36.4)	64 (32.3)	71 (37.6)	68 (44.4)
Agree Strongly	26 (5.0)	42 (9.1)	9 (3.7)	33 (10.2)	22 (11.1)	14 (7.4)	25 (16.3)
Additive Index							
Mean	4.9	5.1	5.0	5.1	4.8	4.9	5.6
Median	5.0	5.0	4.0	5.0	5.0	5.0	6.0
Range	2-8	2-8	2-8	2-8	2-8	2-8	2-8
N	515	460	245	320	198	189	153

Table 5.7 · Adherence to Cultural Prescriptions: Maintaining the Edge

Survey Item	Columbus	Charlotte-Mecklenburg	Portland	Albuquerque	Colorado Springs	Fort Wayne	Knoxville
When I First Arrive On A Scene Or During Any Interaction With A Citizen, I Size Up The Situation In Order To Establish And Maintain Control							
Disagree Strongly	0 (0)	0 (0)	2 (0.8)	2 (0.6)	0 (0)	0 (0)	0 (0)
Disagree Somewhat	6 (1.2)	5 (1.1)	3 (1.2)	7 (2.2)	4 (2.0)	2 (1.1)	1 (0.6)
Agree Somewhat	135 (26.0)	117 (25.2)	80 (32.3)	74 (22.9)	39 (19.6)	58 (30.5)	34 (21.8)
Agree Strongly	379 (72.9)	343 (73.8)	163 (65.7)	240 (74.3)	156 (78.4)	130 (68.4)	121 (77.6)
Mean	3.7	3.7	3.6	3.7	3.8	3.7	3.8
Median	4.0	4.0	4.0	4.0	4.0	4.0	4.0
N	520	465	248	323	199	190	156

Table 5.8 · Adherence to Cultural Prescriptions: Laying Low

Survey Item	Columbus	Charlotte-Mecklenburg	Portland	Albuquerque	Colorado Springs	Fort Wayne	Knoxville
An Officer Is More Effective When S/he Patrols For Serious Felony Violations Rather Than Stopping People For Minor Traffic Violations And Misdemeanors							
Disagree Strongly	123 (24.1)	135 (29.2)	76 (31.5)	100 (31.0)	50 (25.1)	44 (23.3)	44 (28.8)
Disagree Somewhat	297 (58.1)	247 (53.5)	135 (56.0)	157 (48.6)	115 (57.8)	120 (63.5)	80 (52.3)
Agree Somewhat	74 (14.5)	59 (12.8)	22 (9.1)	53 (16.4)	30 (15.1)	22 (11.6)	25 (6.3)
Agree Strongly	17 (3.3)	21 (4.5)	8 (3.3)	13 (4.0)	4 (2.0)	3 (1.6)	4 (2.6)
Mean	2.0	1.9	1.8	1.9	1.9	1.9	1.9
Median	2.0	2.0	2.0	2.0	2.0	2.0	2.0
N	511	462	241	323	199	189	153

Table 5.9 · Adherence to Cultural Prescriptions: Crime Fighter Role Orientation

Survey Items	Columbus	Charlotte-Mecklenburg	Portland	Albuquerque	Colorado Springs	Fort Wayne	Knoxville
Enforcing The Law Is By Far A Patrol Officer's Most Important Responsibility							
Disagree Strongly	12 (2.3)	9 (1.9)	10 (4.0)	8 (2.5)	10 (5.0)	4 (2.1)	2 (1.3)
Disagree Somewhat	99 (19.0)	74 (15.9)	75 (30.4)	62 (19.2)	41 (20.6)	45 (23.7)	19 (12.2)
Agree Somewhat	311 (59.8)	218 (47.0)	131 (53.0)	166 (51.4)	105 (52.8)	117 (61.6)	84 (53.8)
Agree Strongly	98 (18.8)	163 (35.1)	31 (12.6)	87 (26.9)	43 (21.6)	24 (12.6)	51 (32.7)
Most Patrol Officers Have To Spend Too Much of Their Time Handling Unimportant, Non-Crime Calls For Service							
Disagree Strongly	14 (2.7)	17 (3.7)	9 (3.7)	10 (3.1)	9 (4.5)	9 (4.8)	5 (3.3)
Disagree Somewhat	120 (23.2)	90 (19.4)	86 (35.0)	85 (26.2)	42 (21.1)	70 (37.0)	28 (18.3)
Agree Somewhat	281 (54.4)	225 (48.6)	116 (47.2)	182 (56.2)	94 (47.2)	84 (44.4)	83 (54.2)
Agree Strongly	102 (19.7)	131 (28.3)	35 (14.2)	47 (14.5)	54 (27.1)	26 (13.8)	37 (24.2)

Table 5.9 · Adherence to Cultural Prescriptions: Crime Fighter Role Orientation, *cont.*

Survey Items	Columbus	Charlotte-Mecklenburg	Portland	Albuquerque	Colorado Springs	Fort Wayne	Knoxville
Additive Index							
Mean	5.9	6.2	5.5	5.9	5.9	5.5	6.2
Median	6.0	6.0	5.0	6.0	6.0	6.0	6.0
Range	2-8	2-8	2-8	3-8	3-8	3-8	4-8
N	516	461	245	322	199	189	153

Table 5.10 · Adherence to Cultural Prescriptions: Order Maintenance Role Orientation

Survey Items	Columbus	Charlotte-Mecklenburg	Portland	Albuquerque	Colorado Springs	Fort Wayne	Knoxville
Law Enforcement Officers Should Be Required To Do Something About—							
Public Nuisances							
Disagree Strongly	40 (7.8)	64 (13.9)	24 (9.9)	21 (6.5)	21 (10.6)	14 (7.4)	11 (7.2)
Disagree Somewhat	134 (26.0)	122 (26.4)	70 (28.8)	77 (23.8)	70 (35.2)	44 (23.2)	31 (20.3)
Agree Somewhat	278 (53.9)	219 (47.4)	125 (51.4)	179 (55.4)	98 (49.2)	111 (58.4)	92 (60.1)
Agree Strongly	64 (12.4)	57 (12.3)	24 (9.9)	46 (14.2)	10 (5.0)	21 (11.1)	19 (12.4)
Neighbor Disputes							
Disagree Strongly	19 (3.7)	31 (6.7)	24 (9.9)	16 (5.0)	23 (11.6)	7 (3.7)	6 (3.9)
Disagree Somewhat	99 (19.2)	123 (26.6)	82 (33.9)	82 (25.4)	48 (24.2)	38 (20.0)	46 (30.1)
Agree Somewhat	306 (59.4)	236 (51.1)	115 (47.5)	177 (54.8)	102 (51.5)	114 (60.0)	85 (55.6)
Agree Strongly	91 (17.7)	72 (15.6)	21 (8.7)	48 (14.9)	25 (12.6)	31 (16.3)	16 (10.5)

Table 5.10 · Adherence to Cultural Prescriptions: Order Maintenance Role Orientation, *cont.*

Survey Items	Columbus	Charlotte-Mecklenburg	Portland	Albuquerque	Colorado Springs	Fort Wayne	Knoxville
Family Disputes							
Disagree Strongly	16 (3.1)	24 (5.2)	7 (2.9)	5 (1.5)	7 (3.5)	1 (0.5)	4 (2.6)
Disagree Somewhat	71 (13.8)	88 (19.0)	22 (9.1)	16 (4.9)	37 (18.7)	13 (6.8)	22 (14.4)
Agree Somewhat	300 (58.1)	244 (52.7)	99 (40.7)	144 (44.4)	101 (51.0)	94 (49.5)	95 (62.1)
Agree Strongly	129 (25.0)	107 (23.1)	115 (47.3)	159 (49.1)	53 (26.8)	82 (43.2)	32 (20.9)
Additive Index							
Mean	8.7	8.3	8.5	9.0	8.2	9.0	8.5
Median	9.0	8.0	9.0	9.0	8.0	9.0	9.0
Range	3-12	3-12	3-12	3-12	3-12	4-12	3-12
N	513	461	242	323	198	190	153

Table 5.11 Adherence to Cultural Prescriptions: Community Policing Role Orientation

Survey Items	Columbus	Charlotte-Mecklenburg	Portland	Albuquerque	Colorado Springs	Fort Wayne	Knoxville
Law Enforcement Officers Should Be Required To Do Something About— *Litter and Trash*							
Disagree Strongly	67 (12.9)	79 (17.1)	44 (18.1)	33 (10.2)	53 (26.6)	34 (17.9)	21 (13.7)
Disagree Somewhat	171 (33.0)	150 (32.4)	87 (35.8)	84 (25.9)	74 (37.2)	66 (34.7)	55 (35.9)
Agree Somewhat	208 (40.2)	190 (41.0)	88 (36.2)	145 (44.8)	64 (32.2)	78 (41.1)	66 (43.1)
Agree Strongly	72 (13.9)	44 (9.5)	24 (9.9)	62 (19.1)	8 (4.0)	12 (6.3)	11 (7.2)
Parents That Don't Control Their Kids							
Disagree Strongly	52 (10.0)	98 (21.2)	44 (18.2)	52 (16.0)	52 (26.1)	30 (15.8)	37 (24.2)
Disagree Somewhat	156 (30.1)	131 (28.3)	97 (40.1)	127 (39.2)	68 (34.2)	65 (34.2)	59 (38.6)
Agree Somewhat	239 (46.1)	162 (35.0)	73 (30.2)	110 (34.0)	68 (34.2)	79 (41.5)	41 (26.8)
Agree Strongly	71 (13.7)	72 (15.6)	28 (11.6)	35 (10.8)	11 (5.5)	16 (8.4)	16 (10.5)

Table 5.11 · Adherence to Cultural Prescriptions: Community Policing Role Orientation, *cont.*

Survey Items	Columbus	Charlotte-Mecklenburg	Portland	Albuquerque	Colorado Springs	Fort Wayne	Knoxville
Nuisance Businesses							
Disagree Strongly	31 (6.0)	34 (7.3)	26 (10.7)	12 (3.7)	16 (8.0)	18 (9.5)	6 (3.9)
Disagree Somewhat	123 (23.7)	83 (17.9)	49 (20.2)	88 (27.2)	47 (23.6)	56 (29.5)	44 (28.8)
Agree Somewhat	281 (54.2)	253 (54.6)	133 (54.7)	154 (47.5)	100 (50.3)	93 (48.9)	86 (56.2)
Agree Strongly	83 (16.0)	93 (20.1)	35 (14.4)	70 (21.6)	36 (18.1)	23 (12.1)	17 (11.1)
Additive Index							
Mean	8.0	7.7	7.5	8.0	7.1	7.4	7.4
Median	8.0	8.0	8.0	8.0	7.0	7.0	7.0
Range	3-12	3-12	3-12	3-12	3-11	3-12	3-12
N	517	462	242	324	199	190	153

Table 5.12 · Cultural Outcomes: Social Isolation

Survey Items	Columbus	Charlotte-Mecklenburg	Portland	Albuquerque	Colorado Springs	Fort Wayne	Knoxville
Most People Have No Idea How Difficult A Police Officer's Job Is							
Disagree Strongly	3 (0.6)	2 (0.4)	0 (0)	2 (0.6)	1 (0.5)	0 (0)	0 (0)
Disagree Somewhat	26 (5.0)	9 (1.9)	11 (4.5)	12 (3.7)	12 (6.0)	10 (5.3)	3 (1.9)
Agree Somewhat	135 (25.9)	132 (28.3)	66 (26.7)	87 (27.1)	58 (29.1)	67 (35.3)	36 (23.1)
Agree Strongly	357 (68.5)	323 (69.3)	170 (58.8)	220 (68.5)	128 (64.3)	113 (59.5)	117 (75.0)
Given My Choice, When Off Duty, I Would Rather Hang Around With Non-Police Than Other Police Officers							
Agree Strongly	77 (15.2)	92 (20.0)	56 (23.0)	64 (20.0)	41 (20.8)	39 (20.6)	19 (12.4)
Agree Somewhat	214 (42.2)	171 (37.2)	113 (46.5)	117 (36.6)	78 (39.6)	77 (40.7)	52 (34.0)
Disagree Somewhat	198 (39.1)	163 (35.4)	70 (28.8)	116 (36.3)	74 (37.6)	60 (31.7)	67 (43.8)
Disagree Strongly	18 (3.6)	34 (7.4)	4 (1.6)	23 (7.2)	4 (2.0)	13 (6.9)	15 (9.8)

Table 5.12 · Cultural Outcomes: Social Isolation, *cont.*

Survey Items	Columbus	Charlotte-Mecklenburg	Portland	Albuquerque	Colorado Springs	Fort Wayne	Knoxville
In Order To Remain Effective, The Police Officer Should Remain Detached From The Community							
Disagree Strongly	199 (38.7)	158 (34.3)	120 (49.2)	134 (41.5)	97 (48.7)	80 (42.1)	60 (39.2)
Disagree Somewhat	263 (51.2)	248 (53.8)	106 (43.4)	153 (47.4)	87 (43.7)	95 (50.0)	77 (50.3)
Agree Somewhat	47 (9.1)	50 (10.8)	16 (6.6)	28 (8.7)	10 (5.0)	13 (6.8)	15 (9.8)
Agree Strongly	5 (1.0)	5 (1.1)	2 (0.8)	8 (2.5)	5 (2.5)	2 (1.1)	1 (0.7)
Additive Index							
Mean	7.7	7.7	7.3	7.6	7.4	7.5	8.0
Median	8.0	8.0	7.0	8.0	7.0	7.0	8.0
Range	3-11	4-12	5-11	4-11	4-12	4-11	5-10
N	503	457	241	316	197	189	153

Table 5.13 · Cultural Outcomes: Loyalty

Survey Items	Columbus	Charlotte-Mecklenburg	Portland	Albuquerque	Colorado Springs	Fort Wayne	Knoxville
Protecting A Fellow Officer Is One Of My Highest Priorities							
Disagree Strongly	0 (0)	0 (0)	0 (0)	0 (0)	0 (0)	0 (0)	0 (0)
Disagree Somewhat	4 (0.8)	2 (0.4)	2 (0.3)	1 (0.3)	1 (0.5)	1 (0.5)	0 (0)
Agree Somewhat	42 (8.1)	26 (5.6)	22 (8.9)	23 (7.1)	19 (9.5)	12 (6.3)	9 (5.9)
Agree Strongly	473 (91.1)	434 (93.9)	222 (90.2)	300 (92.6)	179 (89.9)	177 (93.2)	144 (94.1)
There Is A Camaraderie And Bond Among Officers That Those Outside Of Policing Would Not Understand							
Disagree Strongly	8 (1.5)	14 (3.0)	5 (2.0)	6 (1.9)	1 (0.5)	1 (0.5)	1 (0.7)
Disagree Somewhat	58 (11.2)	44 (9.5)	30 (12.3)	23 (7.1)	11 (5.5)	15 (7.9)	7 (4.6)
Agree Somewhat	248 (47.9)	189 (41.0)	122 (50.0)	147 (45.5)	95 (47.7)	100 (52.9)	69 (45.1)
Agree Strongly	204 (39.4)	214 (46.4)	87 (35.7)	147 (45.3)	92 (46.2)	73 (38.5)	76 (49.7)

Table 5.13 · Cultural Outcomes: Loyalty, *cont.*

Survey Item	Columbus	Charlotte-Mecklenburg	Portland	Albuquerque	Colorado Springs	Fort Wayne	Knoxville
The Code of Silence Is An Essential Part Of The Mutual Trust Necessary To Good Policing							
Disagree Strongly	102 (20.9)	95 (20.7)	102 (43.2)	56 (18.0)	75 (37.9)	25 (13.4)	30 (19.7)
Disagree Somewhat	233 (47.6)	198 (43.2)	103 (43.6)	119 (38.3)	88 (44.4)	94 (50.5)	59 (38.8)
Agree Somewhat	136 (27.8)	135 (29.5)	27 (11.4)	112 (36.0)	29 (14.6)	57 (30.6)	56 (36.8)
Agree Strongly	18 (3.7)	30 (6.6)	4 (1.7)	24 (7.7)	6 (3.0)	10 (5.4)	7 (4.6)
Additive Index							
Mean	9.3	9.5	8.8	9.6	9.1	9.5	9.7
Median	9.0	10.0	9.0	10.0	9.0	9.0	10.0
Range	5-12	4-12	5-12	6-12	6-12	7-12	5-12
N	487	454	234	309	198	185	149

Table 5.14 · Total Officer Agreement Across Individual Occupational Culture Dimensions

Cultural Dimension	Origin	Number of Survey Items	Threshold for Agreement	Total Agreement
Coercive Authority	Occupational Environment	1	1 of 1	2082 (98.7)
Maintaining the Edge	Coping Mechanism (Occupational)	1	1 of 1	2069 (98.1)
Danger	Occupational Environment	3	2 of 3	2057 (97.5)
Crime Fighter Orientation	Coping Mechanism (Organizational)	2	1 of 2	1943 (92.1)
Loyalty	Outcome (Organizational)	3	2 of 3	1896 (89.9)
Top Management Scrutiny	Organizational Environment	3	2 of 3	1391 (66.0)
Suspiciousness	Coping Mechanism (Occupational)	2	1 of 2	1234 (58.5)
Social Isolation	Outcome (Occupational)	3	2 of 3	961 (45.6)
Community Policing Rejection	Coping Mechanism (Organizational)	3	2 of 3	881 (41.8)
Direct Supervisor Scrutiny	Organizational Environment	2	1 of 2	559 (26.5)
Order Maintenance Rejection	Coping Mechanism (Organizational)	3	2 of 3	489 (23.2)
Laying Low	Coping Mechanism (Organizational)	1	1 of 1	355 (16.8)
Role Ambiguity	Organizational Environment	3	2 of 3	213 (10.1)

Table 5.15 · Culture Carriers: Cumulative Officer Agreement Across All Dimensions and Agencies

Cumulative Cultural Dimension	Columbus	Charlotte-Mecklenburg	Portland	Albuquerque	Colorado Springs	Fort Wayne	Knoxville	Total
Coercive Authority	516 (98.7)	462 (99.1)	244 (97.6)	322 (99.1)	197 (99.0)	186 (97.9)	155 (99.4)	2082 (98.7)
& Maintaining the Edge	512 (97.9)	457 (98.1)	239 (95.6)	313 (96.3)	194 (97.5)	184 (96.8)	154 (98.7)	2053 (97.3)
& Danger	502 (96.0)	449 (96.4)	231 (92.4)	306 (94.2)	191 (96.0)	179 (94.2)	150 (96.2)	2008 (95.2)
& Crime Fighter Orientation	473 (90.4)	429 (92.1)	202 (80.8)	284 (87.4)	179 (89.9)	161 (84.7)	145 (92.9)	1873 (88.9)
& Loyalty	420 (80.3)	394 (84.5)	179 (71.6)	265 (81.5)	173 (86.9)	152 (80.0)	139 (89.1)	1722 (81.7)
& Top Management Disdain	306 (58.5)	239 (51.3)	124 (49.6)	146 (44.9)	118 (59.3)	132 (69.5)	60 (38.5)	1125 (53.3)
& Suspiciousness	190 (36.3)	156 (33.5)	56 (22.4)	91 (28.0)	73 (36.7)	84 (44.2)	48 (30.8)	698 (33.1)
& Social Isolation	99 (18.9)	91 (19.5)	26 (10.4)	50 (15.4)	32 (16.1)	43 (22.6)	30 (19.2)	371 (17.6)
& Community Policing Rejection	45 (8.6)	46 (9.9)	14 (5.6)	19 (5.8)	22 (11.1)	26 (13.7)	14 (9.0)	186 (8.8)
& Direct Supervisory Disdain	10 (1.9)	17 (3.6)	6 (2.4)	9 (2.8)	12 (6.0)	9 (4.7)	2 (1.3)	65 (3.1)

Table 5.15 · Culture Carriers: Cumulative Officer Agreement Across All Dimensions and Agencies, *cont.*

Cumulative Cultural Dimension	Columbus	Charlotte-Mecklenburg	Portland	Albuquerque	Colorado Springs	Fort Wayne	Knoxville	Total
& *Order Maintenance Rejection*	4 (0.8)	9 (1.9)	4 (1.6)	4 (1.2)	9 (4.5)	2 (1.1)	2 (1.3)	34 (1.6)
& *Laying Low*	2 (0.4)	2 (0.4)	2 (0.8)	0 (0.0)	2 (1.0)	0 (0.0)	0 (0.0)	8 (0.4)
& *Role Ambiguity*	0 (0.0)	1 (0.2)	1 (0.4)	0 (0.0)	0 (0.0)	0 (0.0)	0 (0.0)	2 (0.1)
N	523	466	250	325	199	190	156	2109

Table 5.16 · The Role of Police Socialization

Survey Items	Columbus	Charlotte-Mecklenburg	Portland	Albuquerque	Colorado Springs	Fort Wayne	Knoxville
When I Started My Policing Career, Other Officers Were A Valuable Source Of Information On How To Perform As An Officer							
Disagree Strongly	2 (0.4)	0 (0)	2 (0.8)	4 (1.2)	0 (0)	1 (0.5)	0 (0)
Disagree Somewhat	6 (1.2)	7 (1.5)	3 (1.2)	3 (0.9)	3 (1.5)	2 (1.1)	0 (0)
Agree Somewhat	121 (23.2)	107 (23.0)	54 (21.9)	60 (18.6)	37 (18.6)	61 (32.1)	28 (17.9)
Agree Strongly	392 (75.2)	352 (75.5)	188 (76.1)	255 (79.2)	159 (79.9)	126 (66.3)	156 (82.1)
Most Of What I Know About Policing Was Learned "On The Job"							
Disagree Strongly	2 (0.4)	1 (0.2)	1 (0.4)	3 (0.9)	0 (0)	2 (1.1)	3 (2.0)
Disagree Somewhat	21 (4.0)	20 (4.3)	8 (3.3)	23 (7.1)	18 (9.1)	14 (7.4)	17 (11.1)
Agree Somewhat	236 (45.5)	190 (41.2)	107 (43.7)	140 (43.3)	84 (42.4)	110 (58.2)	74 (48.4)
Agree Strongly	260 (50.1)	250 (54.2)	129 (52.7)	157 (48.6)	96 (48.5)	63 (33.3)	59 (38.6)

Table 5.16 · The Role of Police Socialization, *cont.*

Survey Items	Columbus	Charlotte-Mecklenburg	Portland	Albuquerque	Colorado Springs	Fort Wayne	Knoxville
I Try To Teach Younger Officers How To Perform Their Duties As An Officer							
Disagree Strongly	7 (1.4)	8 (1.7)	1 (0.4)	1 (0.3)	3 (1.5)	3 (1.6)	4 (2.6)
Disagree Somewhat	27 (5.3)	27 (5.8)	11 (4.5)	19 (5.9)	11 (5.5)	8 (4.2)	2 (1.3)
Agree Somewhat	282 (55.5)	232 (50.2)	140 (57.9)	159 (49.5)	85 (42.7)	135 (55.6)	78 (51.0)
Agree Strongly	193 (37.9)	195 (42.2)	90 (37.2)	142 (44.2)	100 (50.3)	73 (38.6)	69 (45.1)
Additive Index							
Mean	10.5	10.6	10.6	10.5	10.6	10.2	10.4
Median	11.0	11.0	11.0	11.0	11.0	10.0	10.0
Range	7-12	7-12	6-12	7-12	7-12	6-12	5-12
N	509	459	240	318	198	183	153

Chapter 6

Conclusions and Implications

The aim of this book was to provide a comprehensive understanding of police culture among positions of the hierarchy where it originates (i.e., line-level patrol). In doing so, the preceding chapters focused on various pieces of the multidimensional police culture puzzle. Chapter 1 provided a template for students and researchers to understand the various ways in which culture has been conceptualized, distinguishing four primary perspectives based on key assumptions, foundational research, primary cultural explanation, and common research methodologies. One takeaway message from this chapter was that the most popular conceptualization of police culture is the occupational monolithic perspective. Explanations built on sources of cultural variation by organization, rank, and officer style question the homogeneity among officers purported by occupational accounts. As such, there are competing ideas surrounding the existence of just a single cultural way to cope with the problems and conditions officers face out on the streets and inside the police department. We used this "homogeneity versus heterogeneity" dichotomy as a foundation for exploring the current police culture state of affairs.

In Chapter 2, we provided a unique account of police history in two ways. First, while many texts trace history back to colonial times when policing was a volunteer enterprise, they usually stop or provide very little detail regarding contemporary (i.e., 21st century) approaches. Chapter 2 provided a way for students and scholars to frame (and understand) past, and perhaps more importantly, current operational philosophies of policing. The second contribution of this chapter, which has also yet to be systematically done in any written form, was that we traced (across the five eras) the implications of prevailing operational philosophies for police culture. In doing so, we illustrated how history repeats itself, as well as how the current landscape is ripe for an examination of police culture.

Chapter 3 detailed the internal and external environments of the seven departments that were studied. The utility of this information was that it provided important context regarding where police culture originates. The departments were comparable in that they represented features of similarity found in many American police agencies, while they also offered a degree of variation, especially in terms of size. We used these sizes (i.e., large, mid, and small) as ways to illuminate sources of cultural similarity and dissimilarity in Chapter 5.

Chapter 4 explained the survey methodology that was used to measure and test police culture. Policing students and scholars interested in research methods (in general), and/or survey approaches specifically, would appreciate our documentation of the process of surveying patrol officers. We traced the survey procedure from pre-visit preparation through roll call implementation. This chapter also provided the reader with a detailed account of a variety of assessments of survey success. Perhaps the greatest contribution of Chapter 4 was the "lessons from the field" section, which was designed to complement others who have described systematic social observation (SSO) (Reiss, 1971) and participation observation methods (Van Maanen, 1978).

Chapter 5 put the various pieces of the puzzle, from the prior four chapters, together by examining the multifaceted dimensions of the occupational police culture perspective. In all, 13 constructs from Paoline's (2003) monolithic model were analyzed to assess the extent to which officers from seven departments individually and cumulatively aligned in their perceptions of the work environments, coping mechanisms/cultural prescriptions, and outcomes. Moreover, to the extent that patrol officers deviated from expectations, we explained the ways in which they were diverging (i.e., heterogeneity in orientations or homogeneity in the unexpected direction) and the relevance of agency size and structure. Several interesting findings emerged, which serve as the central focus for the remaining pages of this chapter.

Cultural Homogeneity versus Heterogeneity

A common theme throughout this book has been the distinction between cultural homogeneity (i.e., occupational perspective) and heterogeneity (i.e., organization, rank, and style perspectives). These two competing viewpoints have been a focal point for scholarly debates about police officers for decades. The "winner" (i.e., dominant perspective based on textbook characterizations) has been the occupational version, which is often driven by policing lore over empiricism. By no means is this intended to discredit the seminal police culture work done by the likes of Westley (1970) and Skolnick (1966). Their research discovered police culture, putting the topic on the map for others, in the same way that Kenneth Culp Davis (1969) illuminated discretion. The critique is intended for those who ignore evidence that has demonstrated that not all cops are the same and policing conditions do vary.

At the same time, we understand that it is much more tidy (and convenient) to endorse caricatures of police that stress purely collective features over ways in which they might be occupationally fragmented. Very often the latter approaches, including our most recent work (Ingram, Paoline, & Terrill, 2013), have relied on advanced quantitative techniques that are utilized to efficiently make sense of large data sets and statistical relationships between numerous variables. In the end, such studies may read like "mumbo jumbo" to practitioners or statistically created artifacts to scholars. This is why the current approach conducted straightforward descriptive analyses that focused on getting back to the basics. Even with this in mind, we acknowledge that there is a lot for a reader to digest, which we believe goes with the territory. That is, police culture *is* a complicated beast, even when you employ your best effort to try and simplify it. For those who debate cultural homogeneity versus heterogeneity, we have answers—you are both correct! *Congruent with occupational accounts, we find widespread acceptance of the crime fighting, loyalty, danger, coercive authority, and maintaining the edge features of police culture. We also find unexpected (from occupational versions) cultural homogeneity with respect to perceptions of direct supervisors, laying low, order maintenance functions, and role ambiguity. At the same time, empirical evidence is presented that finds cultural heterogeneity among police in their assessments of citizen suspicion, social isolation, top management, and community policing functions.* What follows is a discussion of this takeaway message.

Cultural Homogeneity

This study finds support for cultural homogeneity across police, although the entire monolithic model was not universally endorsed. That is, just two officers (of the 2109) were true "culture carriers." Interestingly, the cultural dimensions where there was overwhelming agreement among occupational members were some of the same ones that were identified in the very first ethnographic studies of police over half a century ago. These features of occupational culture also coincide with many of the "machismo" characterizations of police officers from researchers and scholars (e.g., Drummond, 1976; Herbert, 1998; Van Maanen, 1974). Moreover, depictions of police in fictional novels (Wambaugh, 1975) and television/movies (Scharrer, 2001) often accentuate these facets. Patrol officers, operating in the 21st century-post 9/11 era of policing, view themselves as a crime fighting, loyal group who have to deal with the danger and use of their coercive power on the streets by being one up on citizens at all times. Officers not only endorse each of these five cultural dimensions individually (i.e., crime fighting, loyalty, danger, coercive authority, and maintaining the edge), but they cumulatively support this constellation of values. Despite minor variation, these cultural outlooks transcend organizational size (and structure), community composition, and geographic locale. In fact, as Chapter 5 demonstrated, we find very little evidence of patterning across these structural features for the cultural orientations of police.

Overall, much of what the founding fathers of police culture researchers described as the dominant features still finds support today. Whether these tenets have remained a consistent part of cultural ethos from 1950 *through* the present is unknown, as several are theoretically counter-productive to the successful implementation of community policing initiatives from the prior era. By contrast, these cultural attributes would fit in rather well with current operational policing philosophies that have revisited many of the ideals of the professional era (i.e., bottom-line, no-nonsense, efficient, crime fighting initiatives). Not coincidently, the original works on police culture were conducted during the height of the professional era. What remains speculative at this juncture is whether the same unintended consequences of operational approaches will result in the current era as what history has told us about the professional era (i.e., separating the police from the public and strengthening the bond among police).

Other evidence of cultural homogeneity is uncovered, although in direct opposition to traditional depictions of police occupational culture. In this sense, we find unexpected widespread agreement among officers. Such differences are reflected in two sets of interrelated cultural orientations. That is, officers generally hold favorable assessments of their direct supervisors and do not express a need to lay low from them (and their scrutiny). In addition, officers are embracing order maintenance patrol functions, in conjunction with their crime fighting ones, and see their role in unambiguous terms. Of particular interest regarding these four cultural departures is they are all facets of the organizational environment. As such, it appears as if the departments that house police officers are quite different from that which was described by foundational cultural research. A few speculative interpretations might explain such dynamics.

In considering the role of history, it could very well be that the changes in the organizational environment (and police culture) are a result of an interaction between operational philosophies of the community era and the current one. The current crime fighting mandates of 21st century policing may be creating clear objectives for the police, thus reducing the ambiguity regarding their role. In short, they are allowing them to concentrate on (and be rewarded for) that which they signed up for in becoming a police officer. At the same time, the policing approaches during the community era documented the benefits of embracing lower level order maintenance objectives before such conditions burgeon into bigger (and more serious) crime issues (Wilson & Kelling, 1982). Street-level patrol officers can interpret order maintenance policing as a "means to an end" whereby such encounters serve as fishing expeditions for stopping citizens and uncovering bigger "traditional" crimes (Kelling & Coles, 1996). In many ways, this can work to undo some of the legal restrictions on police authority by the Supreme Court in the 1960s, enabling officers to get back to the good old days of aggressive crime fighting (Gould & Mastrofski, 2004). In this sense, it may be of little coincidence that officers are embracing both crime fighting and traditional order maintenance objectives.

Another set of related homogenous cultural dimensions is based on the interactions that police have with their immediate supervisors within the organizational environment. The fact that officers are holding favorable attitudes of their immediate supervisors, and not feeling the need to lay low from them, could also be a function of history. Community policing objectives stressed reducing the traditional divisions between units and ranks, with supervisory approaches that were less rule-oriented and encouraged patrol officer creativity and autonomy. In explaining such community policing initiatives, Cordner (1996, p. 9) noted "supervisors should coach and guide their subordinates more, instead of restricting their roles to review of paperwork and enforcement of rules and regulations." Such supervisory approaches could not be more different from the prior professional era, when foundational explanations of police culture noted the tensions between officers and their scrutinizing superiors in the paramilitary organizational environment. Paoline's (2001) police culture study of two departments during the community era found similar positive attitudes of immediate supervisors by patrol officers. It could very well be that remnants of these community policing philosophies are still hanging around departments today or have permanently altered the organizational landscape altogether. Another speculative interpretation is that contemporary patrol supervisors, working within the contemporary crime fighting mandates of the 21st century, are operating more as "street" sergeants (i.e., along *with* patrol officers) and less as "station" sergeants (i.e., strict evaluators *of* patrol officers) (Van Maanen, 1984). From a culture perspective, sergeants may be closer in their supervisory styles to the orientations of street cops versus upper level management cops (Reuss-Ianni, 1983).

Cultural Heterogeneity

While we find homogeneity among police officers for a number of features of police culture, we also find variation. This suggests that elements of the work environments are interpreted (and responded to) with less uniformity among officers. Two sets of interrelated dimensions reflect such heterogeneity.

On the streets, police are divided in their suspicion of citizens and their isolation from them. Community policing advocates would certainly not want officers to be suspicious, and isolated from, their partners in the community. As such, during the prior era there would have been major concern expressed for the contingent of officers that were endorsing suspicion and isolation. Current crime-focused policing proponents would be less concerned with these traditional cultural values, as long as the job is getting done. Such fragmentation in cultural outlooks is not a revelation, as typology research reported similar findings in the 1970s. For example, Brown's (1988) *old-style crime-fighter*, who epitomized the occupational perspective of police culture, was detached from (and suspicious of) citizens, while the *professional* style endorsed polar opposite orientations. Overall, we find that officers are viewing the primary features of the street (i.e., danger and coercive authority) in similar ways, but do not uniformly cope with such conditions by being suspicious of citizens. Moreover, the cumulative impact of the occupational street environment does not equally produce an "us versus them" mentality among contemporary officers.

Within the organization, we find a lack of cultural homogeneity in assessments of top management and orientations toward community policing functions. The division between officers regarding top management is not as equally split as other dimensions, as a large contingent expressed unfavorable attitudes toward these "management cops" (Reuss-Ianni, 1983). That being said, enough officers reported positive views of these organizational leaders to exclude this cultural component from either of the two homogeneity lists. So, while we find cultural differences from past occupational perspective accounts of immediate supervisors (i.e., generally favorable), the same positivity is not extended to more removed top management. Once again, community policing era culture studies reported similar supervisory orientations as what we find here (Paoline, 2001).

Cultural variation, in the organizational environment, is also found for community policing objectives. That is, some officers clearly embrace these functions, while others do not. This finding is also similar to prior police culture research, which found such divisions among the police in the 1990s (Paoline, Myers, & Worden, 2000). It is evident that officers are expanding their role orientations to include traditional order maintenance objectives to complement their crime fighting functions, but only some are willing to push even further to include community policing initiatives. Of interest is that this cultural feature is where we found some patterning by organizational size, as officers from the smallest agencies held the least favorable community policing attitudes, while the two largest were just the opposite. This could very well be a manpower issue, as officers from smaller agencies may not believe they have enough patrol resources to accomplish their crime fighting functions, maintain order, and deal with lower level signs of disorder and decay. On the other hand, larger agencies, with more patrol personnel, might be staffed enough to pursue community policing objectives along with other roles. An alternative explanation is that smaller agencies are able to expedite their orientations from older operational philosophies to more contemporary ones, while for larger departments change takes longer, allowing past ideas to linger. Without multivariate analytical models that control for other theoretically relevant causal factors, these interpretations are merely speculative.

In clarifying how individual-level operational policing styles interact (and coexist) with occupational culture, Brown (1988, p. 85) stated "loyalty and individualism are thus opposite sides of the same coin: the police culture demands loyalty but grants autonomy." It is readily apparent from the preceding discussion that police are loyal to one another. It is also evident that officers share additional constellations of cultural values with one another, some of which are consistent with traditional occupational perspectives (i.e., coercive authority, danger, maintaining the edge, and crime fighting), while others are not (i.e., direct supervisors, laying low, role ambiguity, and order maintenance functions). The individualism that officers are expressing is found in their suspicion and isolation from citizens in the occupational environment. We also see that orientations toward the organizational environment vary, especially with respect to top management and community policing initiatives.

Connotations of Police Culture

Virtually all experts on policing agree that the single greatest obstacle to achieving accountability is the police subculture, and in particular the "code of silence" (Walker, 2001, p. 109).

> The police culture demands of a patrolman unstinting loyalty to his fellow officers, and he receives, in return, protection and honor: a place to assuage real and imagined wrongs inflicted by a (presumably) hostile public; safety from aggressive administrators and supervisors; and the emotional support required to perform a difficult task (Brown, 1988, p. 83).

The above statements capture the positive and negative connotations of police culture. Unfortunately, most of the attention police culture receives focuses on the first connotation. That is, *the* police culture gets blamed for many of the undesirable things that police do (e.g., excessive force, citizen complaints, misuse of authority, rejecting reform efforts, etc.). The bulk of such explanations of the big bad police culture concentrate heavily on the damaging effects of peer loyalty (i.e., "not ratting on fellow officers") and social isolation (i.e., "us versus them")—the two outcomes of the monolithic occupational perspective (Paoline, 2003). At the same time, some degree of separation from the public is inevitable (and perhaps necessary) given the unique position the police hold in terms of their arrest powers and ability to exercise coercion. In addition, the loyalty feature of police culture (i.e., at either micro or macro level) arms officers with the emotional and physical support needed to carry out their policing duties. The cultural balance that must be reached is to ensure that social isolation and loyalty do not manifest into problematic outlooks or behaviors. Given the importance that officers in this study placed on socialization, the right balance starts at the individual level, as police are active learners and teachers. Our findings with respect to social isolation and loyalty shed light on the current state of affairs regarding positive and negative connotations of police culture.

While we found that police collectively agreed on the danger, coercive authority, and need for maintaining the edge dimensions of the occupational (street) environment, we failed to find universal endorsements of social isolation. In fact, many respondents noted that they would rather hang around off-duty with non-police versus their occupational peers. More importantly, while most officers believed that the general public does not understand how difficult their job is, officers uniformly responded that being detached from the community was not needed for effective police work. Overall, these outlooks suggest that contemporary police are fairly well integrated (on their end) with the citizens they are serving.

In terms of loyalty, our findings revealed that officers uniformly place a high priority on protecting their peers. Officers also indicated that there was a camaraderie shared among police that those outside the occupational would not understand. While this collectively points to a close emotional and physical bond among police officers, we also found boundaries to such loyalty. That is, contemporary officers failed to overwhelmingly endorse the "code of silence," which departs drastically from the levels purported by foundational studies of police culture and socialization (Westley, 1970; Van Maanen, 1974).

The cumulative interpretation of our findings, as evidence for purely positive or negative assessments of police culture, depends largely on one's perspective. That is, one could deduce (in a negative manner) that the contingent of officers that endorse certain features of occupational culture (e.g., crime fighting, coercive authority, maintaining the edge, suspiciousness, social isolation, and loyalty) might be susceptible to a variety of abuses of power, while others might view these same outlooks (in a positive manner) as essential attributes of an effective street-cop. Our position is that we should embrace police culture(s) in recognizing the positive properties, and to the extent that negative consequences result from endorsing certain cultural facets, deal with such transgressions accordingly. To universally dichotomize culture as either a good or bad phenomenon is unduly myopic, and will only stunt our ability to fully understand the police.

Moving Forward

Criminologists have long debated the role of nature versus nurture in understanding crime causation. In doing so, a tremendous amount of energy has been expended in providing empirical support regarding whether criminal traits are inherited or socially acquired. Fishbein (1990) has criticized criminologists for focusing on the debate, which she asserts has limited the growth of the field. That is, researchers fixate on their side of the argument, often ignoring all of the evidence (or any contribution) from the opposing camp. In mediating the two sides, Fishbein has called for a more balanced approach that acknowledges and appreciates the scientific contributions of the disparate viewpoints. As such, she concludes that instead of a nature versus nurture dichotomy, criminologists should endorse a nature plus nurture perspective. Fishbein's recommendations for the field were supported by empirical research, illustrating how one's biological properties and sociological environment interact to produce behavior. Based on the evidence that has been provided in this book, along with prior research, we propose a similar approach for studies of police culture. That is, culture does not have to be a homogeneity versus heterogeneity proposition, but instead should be treated as homogeneity *and* heterogeneity.

It is our hope that culture remains on the radar of those studying the police. We welcome additions to the work that was presented here. Also, we encourage those interested in police culture to be creative, regardless of the research method(s) employed. Creativity comes from rolling up your sleeves and immersing yourself in the subject matter. Creativity also comes from taking chances. A creative study of police culture will undoubtedly include getting into a variety of police departments and digging around. Cultural digging will occur by talking, interviewing, surveying, and observing line-level personnel, specialized units, middle managers, and chief executives. Researchers should continue to search for empirical evidence of past notions, but more importantly keep your eyes peeled for new ideas. In short, challenge traditional police culture thoughts, including what we have presented here. That is, expand the environments, elements of the environments, coping mechanisms, and outcomes. Policing has undergone numerous changes since the 1950s, and additions to the culture model are needed.

Moving forward should also include efforts to tease out the explanatory factors that account for cultural variation among officers. We documented where such variation is taking place, explaining it will provide much needed insight into the dynamics that influence segmentation. Past work, including some of our own, has yet to consistently find empirical evidence regarding theoretically relevant demographic factors (e.g., sex, race, education, experience, etc.), although there is burgeoning research that has illuminated the importance of other policing features such as: shift, beat, and workgroup (e.g., Paoline, 2001; Ingram et al., 2013). Further disentangling these causal mechanisms would add to the police culture knowledge base. Overall, let us move beyond the "easy" classifications of culture and test the limits of our ideas about the practically and scholarly relevant notions of homogeneity and heterogeneity. The base has been provided here; we urge researchers to build on it. We refrain from providing the traditional "research directions" roadmap that is found in the typical peer reviewed journal article, as this would fly in the face of the intended message of individual creativity.

Research pursuits into creative police culture inquiries would probably best be suited for doctoral students as part of their dissertations. We say this for a few basic reasons. First, doctoral students have the adventurous energy needed for such endeavors, while at the same time are not pressed for absolute, immediate results. A doctoral dissertation is more about the research process over the actual outcome. That is, dissertation success depends on executing the committee-approved plan of action and not finding statistically significant regression coefficients. This flexibility would allow a doctoral student to take more chances in the field, worrying less about statistical findings and concentrating more on substantive relationships. By contrast, tenure seeking assistant professors do not get published for the research process. Moreover, the overall pressure to publish and seek (and acquire) external funding by contemporary universities has created a work environment where creative police culture research might be too much of a gamble for the untenured assistant professor. In large part, this has stymied much of the theoretical development by young criminology and criminal justice scholars. If one were to comprehensively answer all of the police culture questions and were to publish it in the *American Sociological Review* journal or as an *Oxford University Press* book, that would represent just one publication (albeit heavily weighted) among the many needed toward promotion and tenure. Related to what we have covered in this book, this is a college professor culture issue! Doctoral students, on the other hand, only need that one dissertation publication to successfully complete their degrees. Westley (1970) and Paoline (2001) were cultural works that were both based on doctoral dissertations. These serve as illustrations that it has been done before.

Professors at the associate and full level are in positions where there are fewer bottom-line, time-specified, publishing and grant-related expectations, although both might be less likely to take on the risks needed for a full-scale study of police culture. By these stages in one's career research interests have been formulated, and few (to date) have demonstrated that they are late bloomers to the culture area. The energy and vigor needed to tackle the subject matter, for many, may not be there, and mid- and senior-level professors are better situated for doing the leg work in setting projects up versus getting in the trenches. Creative culture studies are not conducted by calling agencies requesting all electronic data or by a single day visit to a police department. Where the efforts of associate and full professors would be best served is in a supervisory position directing the doctoral students, keeping them on a general research path, yet allowing them to meander in the name of creativity. To use a hiking analogy, some of the most interesting things seen in the woods are discovered by less experienced hikers who wander into areas where no one has gone or believed would be fruitful. Mid- and senior-level directors would be invaluable in gaining access to a police department(s) for students, or allowing them to study culture as part of an existing research project.

Finally, in moving forward, we make a general plea to funding sources that routinely convene police practitioners and academics to discuss the importance of understanding the causes and consequences of police culture—*put your money where your mouth is!* Simply providing a government document summarizing the workshop's proceedings; listing participants (many of whom are the "usual suspects" and not engaged in police culture research); and recommending research directions, has does little to advance the area. Such ideas usually die as soon as the meeting is over. Rarely, if ever, are the recommendations carried out with external funding support. Moreover, the messages from such roundtables often do more harm than good. For example, most of those who participate speak of police culture in exclusively negative terms (i.e., as impediments to successful reform, accountability, and integrity) without considering the complexities of culture, including the positive dimensions. We implore academics, practitioners, and students to avoid such one-dimensional thinking about a multifaceted and dynamic aspect of American policing.

References

Brown, M. K. (1988). *Working the street: Police discretion and the dilemmas of reform*. New York: Russell Sage Foundation.

Cordner, G. (1996). *Principles and elements of community policing*. Washington, DC: Office of Community Oriented Policing Services, U.S. Department of Justice.

Davis, K. C. (1969). *Discretionary justice*. Baton Rouge, LA: Louisiana State University Press.

Drummond, D. S. (1976). *Police culture*. Beverly Hills, CA: Sage.

Fishbein, D. H. (1990). Biological perspectives in criminology. *Criminology, 28*, 27–72.

Gould, J. B., & Mastrofski, S. D. (2004). Suspect searches: Assessing police behavior under the U.S. Constitution. *Criminology and Public Policy, 3*, 315–362.

Herbert, S. (1998). Police subculture reconsidered. *Criminology, 36*, 343–370.

Ingram, J. R., Paoline, E. A., III, & Terrill, W. (2013). A multilevel framework for understanding police culture: The role of the workgroup. *Criminology, 51*, 365–398.

Kelling, G. L., & Coles, C. M. (1996). *Fixing broken windows: Restoring order and reducing crime in our communities*. New York, NY: Simon & Schuster.

Paoline, E. A., III. (2001). *Rethinking police culture: Officers' occupational attitudes*. New York, NY: LFB Publishing.

Paoline, E. A., III. (2003). Taking stock: Toward a richer understanding of police culture. *Journal of Criminal Justice, 31*, 199–214.

Paoline, E. A., III, Myers, S. M., & Worden, R. E. (2000). Police culture, individualism, and community policing: Evidence from two police departments. *Justice Quarterly, 17*, 575–605.

Reiss, A. J. Jr. (1971). Systematic observation of natural social phenomena. In H. L. Costner (Ed.), *Sociological methodology* (pp. 3–33). San Francisco, CA: Jossey-Bass Inc.

Reuss-Ianni, E. (1983) *Two cultures of policing*. New Brunswick, NJ: Transaction.

Scharrer, E. (2001). Tough guys: The portrayal of hypermasculinity and aggression in televised police dramas. *Journal of Broadcasting & Electronic Media, 45,* 615–634.

Skolnick, J. H. (1966). *Justice without trial: Law enforcement in democratic society*. New York: John Wiley.

Van Maanen, J. (1974). Working the street: A developmental view of police behavior. In H. Jacob (Ed.), *The potential for reform of criminal justice* (pp. 83–128). Beverly Hills, CA: Sage.

Van Maanen, J. (1978). Epilogue on watching the watchers. In P. K. Manning & J. Van Maanen (Eds.), *Policing: A View from the Streets* (pp. 309–349). New York, NY: Random House.

Van Maanen, J. (1984). Making rank: Becoming an American police sergeant. *Urban Life, 13,* 155–176.

Walker, S. (2001). *Police accountability: The role of citizen oversight*. Belmont, CA: Wadsworth.

Wambaugh, J. (1975). *The choirboys*. New York, NY: Dell Publishing.

Westley, W. A. (1970). *Violence and the police: A sociological study of law, custom, and morality*. Cambridge, MA: MIT Press.

Wilson, J. Q., & Kelling, G. (1982). Broken windows: The police and neighborhood safety. *The Atlantic Monthly,* 29–38.

Index

Note: *t* indicates table. "Research" following names indicates scholars whose research is discussed.